AND THE
PAPAS

THE
NANAS
AND THE
PAPAS

A BOOMERS'
GUIDE TO
GRANDPARENTING

Kathryn and Allan Zullo

Andrews McMeel
Publishing

Kansas City

www.andrewsmcmeel.com

98 99 00 01 02 RDH 10 9 8 7 6 5 4 3 2 1

Library of Congress Cataloging-in-Publication Data

Zullo, Kathryn.
    The nanas and the papas : a boomers' guide to grandparenting / Kathryn and Allan Zullo.
        p.   cm.
    Includes bibliographical references (p.).
    ISBN 0-8362-6787-7 (pbk.)
    1. Grandparenting—United States. 2. Baby boom generation— United States. 3. Grandparents—United States—Family relationships. 4. Grandparent and child—United States. I. Zullo, Allan. II. Title.
HQ759.9.Z85   1998
306.874'5—dc21   98-24174
                                                                                CIP

Composed by Kelly & Company, Lee's Summit, Missouri

ATTENTION: SCHOOLS AND BUSINESSES

Andrews McMeel books are available at quantity discounts with bulk purchase for educational, business, or sales promotional use. For information, please write to: Special Sales Department, Andrews McMeel Publishing, 4520 Main Street, Kansas City, Missouri 64111.

This is dedicated to the ones we love—
our grandsons Chad and Danny and
(hopefully) any future grandchildren.

Contents

Contents

Acknowledgments

We are extremely grateful for the assistance of all the experts who shared with us their research, comments, and advice.

This book could not have been completed without the cooperation, understanding, and encouragement of the guru of grandparents, Arthur Kornhaber, M.D., founder of the Foundation for Grandparenting.

We also wish to thank the following experts for answering our questions in lengthy, personal interviews: Barbara Bowman, president of the Erikson Institute; T. Berry Brazelton, M.D., noted author and pediatrician; Perry Buffington, Ph.D., psychologist and syndicated columnist; Susan Ginsberg, Ed.D., editor and publisher of *Work & Family Life*; Jody Martin, curriculum specialist for the Children's World Learning Centers; Peter Martin, Ph.D., professor of human development and family studies at Iowa State University; Susan Newman, Ph.D., sociologist and author; Gregory F. Sanders, Ph.D., associate professor of child development and family relations at North Dakota State University; and attorney Richard Victor, executive director of the Grandparents Rights Organization.

In addition, we appreciate the help of the following: Daniel E. Clement and Pat Connolly, who granted permission to quote from their Web pages; Jane Curry, of the Erikson Institute; David

Acknowledgments

Fenech, president and executive director of PRIORITY '90s: A Community Roundtable for Genesee County's Children & Families; Whitney Gilman, of the Children's World Learning Centers; Jay Goodman, executive director of the Foundation for Grandparenting; Nita Marlow; John McLain, president of McLain Communications; Martha Moffett; and Jeffery Wallem, CFP, of the Wallem Associates.

We especially want to thank all the nanas and papas who took the time to share with us their thoughts, experiences, and suggestions.

THE
NANAS
AND THE
PAPAS

Introduction

Sunshine, Lollipops, and Rainbows

"Mom, Dad," said our daughter, Allison, over the speakerphone. "How would you like to be called by different names?"

"Like what," we asked. "The Captain and Tennille?"

"No," Allison replied. "Something more along the lines of . . ." She paused for dramatic effect. ". . . Nana and Papa."

"Oh, my God!" we roared. "You're pregnant!"

"Yes, you're going to be grandparents!"

Thrilled by the news, we happily pictured all the fun we would have with our first grandchild—showering him with love, plying him with forbidden treats behind his parents' backs, taking him hiking and canoeing, and buying him the hippest clothes. (We guessed the child would be a boy because our son-in-law, Dan, came from a family of five boys.)

But then we experienced a slight moment of panic. What did we really know about being grandparents? We were active forty-somethings—nothing like the stereotypical gray-haired grandmas and grandpas who sat in rocking chairs, baked cookies, whittled toys, and told stories of the "good old days." We weren't like the Ensure-swilling senior citizens or the frumpy, wrinkled elderly neighbors so often portrayed in TV commercials and movies.

Kathy (reminiscing about her childhood visits with her grandmother Melba Lang): *"I would wake up in my grandparents' farmhouse to the smell of fresh cinnamon rolls baking in the oven. In the afternoon I'd find a batch of Grandma's homemade cookies cooling on the rack. She made bread from scratch and picked vegetables from her garden. After a week at Grandma's I would go home with a sweater that she had knit by hand. She had twenty-six grandchildren—and she made every one of them sweaters when they came to visit.*

"I adored my grandmother. I always thought everyone should have a grandma like mine. But I can't be like her. I don't bake cookies. I don't knit sweaters. I don't grow my own veggies. I don't have time, with all the work and travel I do. What kind of a grandmother is that?"

Allan: *"My grandparents died before I was old enough to remember them. My role models were fashioned from TV—a cross between Grandpa McCoy and Grandpa Munster."*

We are the typical boomer nana and papa—younger, healthier, wealthier, and better educated than our grandparents were. We are more active and less formal than our own parents were at our age. We no longer fit the traditional yet unrealistic image of our elderly kin, who lived in a different period. Most boomer grandparents work hard and lead vigorous, often stressful lives where time is a valuable commodity.

Many of us experiencing the nana and papa role for the first time must deal with issues far removed from what our grandparents faced. Our adult children's ideas of child rearing are often very different from the views of Dr. Spock, to which we once pledged allegiance. Millions of boomers must help raise the grandkids because of economic pressures or personal problems of their adult children. Other factors, such as living in far-flung communities and coping with divorce, make it more of a challenge for boomers to play a meaningful part in our grandchildren's lives.

For way too many kids, the family life typified by the Cleavers, Stones, and Andersons can be experienced only on Nick at Nite. The Census Bureau says that only about half of American children live in traditional families where Mom and Dad preside over the nuclear brood.

Today, we have families that are blended, broken, strained, and strapped. When we were kids, new friends asked each other, "What does your father do for a living?" Now the question asked is, "Does your dad live with you?" Children are far more likely to live with a never-married mother than we boomers were. In 1970, 7 percent of kids living with one parent were being raised by a parent who had never wed. Now it's 33 percent.

In increasing numbers, adult children who are either drugged out, wiped out, or stressed out have shown up on their parents' doorsteps and said, "Here, take care of my kids." Six percent of all children today—about four million—are living in their grandparents' homes, according to the Population Reference Bureau.

And there's another challenge facing today's boomer grandparents. For the first time in history, a generation of grandparents will be caring for their parents. We boomers must find ways to handle our lives while providing help for our elderly parents as well as for our adult children and grandchildren.

Child rearing has changed so much since we raised our kids. There are new rules about what to do and not to do. That old crib you saved for the day you became a grandparent must be thrown out because the rails are too far apart. The baby quilt you wanted to hand down is a no-no—at least until the child is much older. That old windup swing with the chains? Throw it away. The baby's fingers can get caught in the mechanism.

There's so much to learn (and unlearn) now: Don't put the baby on her tummy for a nap, Nana; put her on her back. Toss out the baby aspirin, Papa; use children's ibuprofen instead. No, Grammy, don't give the baby any juice; it's not good for her at this age.

But some things haven't changed—like the incredible joy and unconditional love grandparents and grandchildren share. It's like sunshine, lollipops, and rainbows.

> **Allan:** *"When Kathy held our first grandson, Chad, for the first time, I noticed that her teary smile and sweet murmurs mimicked those she gave our children at their births. I knew instantly she'd make a great nana.*
>
> *"When I finally wrested the baby out of her arms and cradled him in mine, I gazed at my daughter, Allison, and then at my father. Here together in one room was the spectrum of my life—four generations bound by blood and love. I wanted to say something profound and meaningful; words from deep within my soul; a declaration that Allison would record for posterity in Chad's baby book. I gently kissed Chad on the forehead and announced, 'Awesome!' I'll never forgive myself for such a lame remark. However, a fellow granddad consoled me by claiming that grandkids have a way of turning your mind to mush."*

We are determined to become the best grandparents possible by relying on our hearts, our instincts, and the confidence that we'll do a good job. But life, families, and roles are so different now than when our grandparents and parents were tending to their grandkids. Hoping to get a little guidance, we headed to the bookstores shortly after Chad was born. We searched for a book on grandparenting aimed at our generation, a guide that would offer tips and suggestions helpful to us.

We found several fine books written by experts. But they dealt with older grandparents who had time on their hands and money in their pockets. Almost all the books were warmhearted memoirs, detailed studies, or straight how-tos for the retired grandparent. Although many of the experts' tips certainly made sense for nanas and papas of any age and any generation, we still couldn't find a book that spoke directly to us—boomer grandparents.

How does the boomer cope with the changing dynamics of today's family? Deal with new parenting techniques and baby products? Spend quality time with the grandkids while still pursuing work and enjoying pastimes?

That's when we decided to write *The Nanas and the Papas*. It's geared toward expectant boomer grandparents and those with infant or toddler grandkids. For the book, we sought out experts who offered current research, tips, suggestions, and experiences that were relevant to young nanas and papas.

We interviewed the guru of grandparents, Arthur Kornhaber, M.D., founder of the Foundation for Grandparenting. He and his wife, Carol, initiated the Grandparent Study to systematically investigate the grandparent-grandchild relationship—research that continues to this day. Dr. Kornhaber, a grandpa who since 1970 has been a tireless champion for grandparent involvement in family life, graciously answered our questions and allowed us to quote from his studies.

We also interviewed grandmother and respected educator Barbara Bowman, president of the Chicago-based Erikson Institute for the Advanced Study of Child Development, which is a private graduate school and research center; T. Berry Brazelton, M.D., the internationally renowned pediatrician, author of *Touchpoints: Your Child's Emotional and Behavioral Development*, founder of the Child Development Unit of Children's Hospital in Boston, cofounder of the national advocacy group Parent Action, and a grandfather; Perry (Doctor Buff) Buffington, Ph.D., noted family psychologist, syndicated columnist, and fellow boomer; Susan

Ginsberg, Ed.D., editor and publisher of the national newsletter *Work & Family Life* and a grandmother; Jody Martin, curriculum specialist for the Children's World Learning Centers, a nationwide child care provider; Peter Martin, Ph.D., professor of human development and family studies at Iowa State University and a fellow boomer; Susan Newman, Ph.D., sociologist, author, and grandmother; Gregory F. Sanders, Ph.D., associate professor of child development and family relations at North Dakota State University; attorney Richard Victor, executive director of the Grandparents Rights Organization; and Jeffrey Wallem, noted certified financial planner.

In addition, we gathered informative and wry observations, advice, and accounts from other boomer nanas and papas through personal interviews, e-mail, and various grandparent and boomer Web sites. Their comments are scattered throughout the book. In most cases, we used their real names or their e-mail nicknames. But in a few sensitive cases, some names were changed to protect their identity. (Comments labeled from Kathy or Allan are from us, the authors.)

The book also features an appendix in the back with resources that might prove helpful. It includes Web sites, e-mail and snail-mail addresses, and phone numbers of grandparenting organizations, support groups, and newsletters, as well as recommended reading.

Now more than ever, grandparent involvement is vital to the stability and welfare of grandchildren from the moment they take their first breath. Balancing hectic lives of hard work and hard play with the needs of our grandchildren, we boomers could use a little guidance if we are to become the coolest, most understanding, and loving grandparents of the twenty-first century. Through the advice of experts and the experiences of fellow boomers, we hope *The Nanas and the Papas* will help you enjoy to the fullest your new grand job.

Talking 'bout Our Generation

The Boomers' Newest Gig

It's hard to believe, isn't it? We, the generation that defined youth—that embraced it and obsessed over it—are now becoming *grandparents.*

Many of us are once again hearing the pitter-patter of little feet as the first wave of our 76-million-member generation hits the half-century mark. Those tiny feet are multiplying into a resounding beat as more and more of our kids are having kids. Now it's our turn to grandparent. By the year 2005, according to the National Institute on Aging, there will be an estimated eighty million grandparents—and, says *American Demographics,* nearly half will be baby boomers.

Let's face it, boomers rule. (Maybe not very well, but we do rule.) We represent more than a quarter of the U.S. population. And whether we like it or not, we're aging—a boomer turns fifty every seven seconds. We've gone from love beads to love handles; Volkswagen vans to minivans; rollerskates to Rollerblades. The songs we once grooved to now sell hamburgers, cars, eyeglasses, soda, and beer.

We no longer can say time is on our side. And yet it doesn't seem that long ago when the pitter-patter of little feet was ours. We were the Spock babies doted on by stay-at-home moms in an era when fear was red and war was cold. We went to grade school in the shadow of the H-bomb and saw the fallout of Rosa Parks's courageous "No." We didn't know the answer to the $64,000 Question, but we did to "Hey, kids, what time is it?" We fell in love with Elvis, Annette, and James. We hula-hooped and did the twist. We were moved by Dr. King's dream. We were shocked by a national nightmare that stole our collective innocence one grim November day in Dallas. We flipped out over the Beatles and the Stones. We tuned in, turned on, and dropped out. We participated in be-ins, sit-ins, and love-ins. We went from the Summer of Love to the Days of Rage. We spilled our blood in Watts, Chicago, Kent State, and the jungles of Vietnam. We burned draft cards and bras. We came together on Max Yasgur's farm. We discovered Nixon was a crook and Jesus was a superstar. We were stayin' alive in discos. We had to imagine life without John Lennon . . . and life with Ronald Reagan. We were plugging in our new PCs. We raised a generation of MTV junkies and tried to keep them from the same youthful exuberances that we had enjoyed at their age. We climbed StairMasters and corporate ladders only to watch many of us fall off later. We waged war against AIDS, crack, homelessness, and racism (arguably too little, too late). We laughed with Roseanne and with Seinfeld. We jacked up the rates of drunk driving, suicide, illegitimate births, crime, and drug use. We visited the Bridges of Madison County and rooted for Thelma and Louise. And while we sent our kids out into the real world, we sent our first fellow boomer (crop of '46) to the White House.

To use a phrase from our past, what a rush!

Yet our life's journey is far from over. We boomers are now embarking on a new adventure—perhaps the most fun trip of all—as grandparents. What are we to make of this new gig? To get a clue on how we as a generation will handle this role, we need to look back at the way we were. Our history—in terms of what happened to us and what we made happen—is part of our makeup that will influence our effectiveness as family elders.

Think back. From the contented '50s to the revolutionary '60s to the discontented '70s to the booming '80s to the mellow '90s, what national event had the biggest impact on your life? In a survey of fifty-year-old boomers conducted by *New Choices* magazine, the Vietnam War (38 percent), the assassination of John F. Kennedy (25 percent), and the social movements of the time (20 percent) were the newsmakers that affected our generation the most, shaping our values, beliefs, and attitudes.

In their enlightening book *Generations*, cultural historians William Strauss and Neil Howe say that boomers have morphed

> from Beaver Cleaver to hippie to bran-eater to yuppie to what some are calling "Neo-Puritan" in a manner quite unlike what anyone, themselves included, ever expected. . . . [Boomers have] outlived any number of temporary labels: Dr. Spock, Pepsi, Rock, Now, Sixties, Love, Protest, Woodstock, Vietnam, Me, Big Chill, Yuppie and Post Yuppie Generation.
>
> From VJ Day forward, whatever age bracket Boomers have occupied has been the cultural and spiritual focal point for American society as a whole. Through their childhood, America was child-obsessed; in their youth, youth-obsessed; in their yuppie phase, yuppie-obsessed. . . . Arriving as the inheritors of G.I. triumph, Boomers have always seen their mission not as constructing a society, but of justifying, even sanctifying it.
>
> This mixture of high self-esteem and selective self-indulgence has at once repelled and fascinated other generations, giving Boomers a reputation for grating arrogance—and for transcendent cultural wisdom.

Now we're entering grandparenthood in a world far different from what our grandmas and grandpas faced at this stage of life. At the turn of the twenty-first century, we boomers are in our prime, earning good money, enjoying good health. We're the best-educated, most active, and youngest older generation ever. Of fifty-year-old boomers, reports the *New Choices* survey, 96 percent are high school graduates and 73 percent have attended college or technical school. More than half are in two-income households with family earnings of $65,000 or more. Eighty percent are employed full-time, another 10 percent part-time. Eighty percent are married.

As obsessed as boomers are with youth, the survey found that a surprising 73 percent say the half-century milestone doesn't faze them. Part of the reason for such a positive attitude is that they simply don't feel their age. Many boomers imagine themselves to be fifteen years younger than they really are. (That's why some have admitted trouble coming to grips with being a grandparent.)

However, many of us are feeling the strain of being pulled in different directions. Our adult children need us. Our elderly parents need us. Our employers need us. Our spouses need us. Our friends need us. We worry about breast cancer and prostate cancer. We worry about money—not having enough to retire (that still seems so far away) or to maintain our current lifestyle.

We have seen how downsizing, drugs, and divorce have severely stressed many families. Support systems that we took for granted when we were growing up—school, church, neighbors, extended family—are no longer as effective in helping parents raise their children.

"When you look at demographic data for people in their late forties moving into their fifties . . . this is a stage when there is a lot of family transition going on and, in a sense, a recasting of obligations across generations," says Peter Morrison, a demographer at Rand Corporation, a nonprofit research institution.

Now more than ever, we are realizing how vital grandparents are not only to the well-being of the family but to the well-being of the country.

So, what kind of nanas and papas will we boomers be? We might be the most self-absorbed, materialistic, spoiled generation of the millennium, but unless the experts are blowing smoke, we will be pretty good grandparents who likely will:

- reinvent and welcome grandparenthood
- fret over finding the time to care for our aging parents and to enjoy our grandchildren
- become conservative, caring elders
- parlay grandparenthood into a second chance at righting whatever wrongs we made as parents
- take a proactive role in helping and advising our adult children

"The boomers are not a passive generation," says Arthur Kornhaber, M.D., founder of the Foundation for Grandparenting. "They are going to say, 'I want to explore this new stage of life.' Of course, some boomers will say, 'I don't want to be old.' But I think most will want to be immortalized. And they're going to discover, 'I can immortalize myself by leaving my soul with a child.'"

Famed pediatrician T. Berry Brazelton believes we'll learn from our mistakes. "I think the baby boomers will make good grandparents," he declares.

Boomers likely will raise the consciousness of society regarding the important role that grandparents play. It's only natural for us boomers to alter the country's attitudes and beliefs. Call it egocentric if you want, but it's the truth. We've been doing it our whole lives.

"We have been nothing if not forceful in terms of our impact," boomer journalist Peggy Noonan wrote in *New Choices.* "We are and have been the most significant demographic fact of American life in all of American history: We changed, in our youth, the culture of a great nation, sweeping it with our music, our movies, our art and styles and tastes in entertainment. Our assumptions about sex changed the sexual landscape. We altered our country's political climate when we decided to oppose a war, changing American attitudes about our government in the process."

Can there be any doubt that as our children have children we will redefine grandparenthood? We will make it up as we go along. That's been our style, and it's not likely to change. We are the hippest nanas and papas ever. "Do you realize we are going to have a generation of Grandma Heathers?" says Perry Buffington, Ph.D., a boomer and noted psychologist. "The image and concept of grandparents are changing."

Society may be reluctant to let go of the stereotypical picture of the gray-haired, cane-wielding grandparent, but as the number of boomer nanas and papas steadily increases, a new image will more closely reflect reality.

We will rage against age and try to make grandparenting cool, says Dr. Kornhaber. "The new grandparent will have to be reinvented. We don't have any precedent for this. I have enough faith in the boomers and their ability to avoid hanging their hats on outmoded concepts of grandparenting."

Adds Peter Martin, professor of human development and family studies at Iowa State University, "Boomers by and large think they've done a great job in affecting society since the sixties. They've always believed they were fighting for a cause." Now as boomers age, he believes we will fight to make grandparenting important. "I predict boomer grandparents will define their role in more certain terms and I think they'll do a good job."

Dr. Martin, a boomer himself, believes members of our generation will be pioneers in grandparenting because we are educating ourselves about our role and how we relate to the family. "Our

healthy, active lives will translate into much stronger relationships with our grandchildren."

> **Glen (Pee Paw) Reed:** *"My grandsons are five and
> three and they light up my heart like nothing else I have
> experienced in my forty-seven years. They beam at my
> approach and I beam at theirs. The love almost defies
> explanation and transcends time and the explanations
> that other relationships require."*

Although many critics claim boomers aren't, or won't be, interested in being there for their grandkids, most studies indicate
that boomers—even those who cherish their independence and
autonomy—want to spend as much time as possible with their
grandchildren.

Increasing numbers are shedding the yuppie life. Fewer than
half of boomers say that achieving the American Dream means
"looking young," "being wealthy," or "having power and influence,"
according to a survey conducted by Roper Starch Worldwide, Inc.
While our parents defined the American Dream from the outside
in, boomers tend to define it from the inside out.

Despite all the talk of materialism, we boomers tend to measure
ourselves by the spiritual strength within. In one study, boomer
males were asked to compare themselves with their fathers at the
same phase of life. By an overwhelming nine-to-one ratio, boomers
said their lives were more meaningful.

In the *New Choices* boomer survey, nearly 40 percent say religion has become more important to them over the course of their
lives. Nearly 60 percent think their values have remained fairly
constant over time. Although half the people surveyed say that
material success and comforts have become more important to
them, a majority say they still feel a personal responsibility to
make the world a better place. The survey also found that 81 per-

cent see the coming years as a time for new opportunities, including spending more time with their families.

However, other studies show that the number of long-distance grandparents is increasing.

Whether or not we become effective nanas and papas will depend largely upon how we deal with the social, economic, and personal issues that affect us as we age.

"Boomers are going to have to learn how to be balanced in this phase of their lives," says Dr. Kornhaber. "They will still be quite active with their jobs and leisure time. Yet they will have a very broad range of family roles to play—mother, father, daughter, son, sister, brother, grandmother, and grandfather. They need to figure out how to balance these priorities.

"We are given twenty extra years of life. I am in my sixties and I run every morning. When my grandfather was my age he was totally burned out. Aging is a bewildering kind of thing. The next generation is going to go through this same kind of bewilderment. At the same time, it's exciting. Rather than take another job for money, I hope we get back to making sure we can help our children and grandchildren. This is especially true of boomer men who were not there as fathers."

> **Bob (Boppy) Giavonni:** *"I thought it was rewarding to be a father, but being a grandpa is a gas!"*

Work still will remain a major part of the lives of boomer grandparents. One forecasting firm, NPA Data Services, predicts that boomer men will be less likely than their fathers to take early retirement. Not only that, but boomer women will stay in the labor force at least as long as men do.

"There's no denying that people are retiring at a much later date," says prominent educator Barbara Bowman. "The availability of grandparents as a support system has, in many cases, decreased because they are engaged actively in the workforce. Although the emotional support that grandparents are supposed to give their children and grandchildren may continue, very often it doesn't consist of their presence."

However, flex time at the office and telecommuting at home are offering many boomer nanas and papas more opportunities to spend needed time with their grandkids. But, because Americans are living longer, many boomers also worry about the well-being of their retired parents and the possibility of big hospital and nursing-care bills.

"The boomers are the first generation in large numbers to become grandparents while their parents are still alive," says Dr. Martin. "You'll have multiple caregiving roles. You are involved in your children's and grandchildren's lives as well as your parents'. Who is going to provide for your elderly parents' needs and help out your adult children? When are you going to visit your parents? When are you going to see your grandchildren? These are issues which you must confront."

Boomer grandparents who are fit and enjoy an active lifestyle will influence their grandchildren, Dr. Martin adds. "You may have a more active grandparenting style and not be someone who visits only on birthdays and holidays. I envision a grandparent who takes the grandchildren on travels and exposes them to new experiences. Much depends on how economically secure boomers will be. The verdict is still out.

"I hear two stories. One says that boomers aren't saving enough for retirement. If that's true, visits will be limited because you won't be able to afford trips to the grandchildren. On the other hand, I hear that we will inherit quite a bit of money. If that's correct, then we'll have the resources to do the fun things that we didn't spend enough time or money on with our own kids. Boomers could get very close to their grandchildren. I can see the day when grandkids do things with their grandparents that they won't do with their own parents."

Dr. Martin believes aging boomers will not want to live in a multigenerational household. "People don't want to live that way unless it's a crisis or emergency. I hope we don't have to make that choice. What we want is 'intimacy at a distance.' We want to be close to our kids and grandkids but we don't want to live under one roof. We want our own life to be under our control."

Boomer grandparents definitely will complain about not having enough time for all the things they want to do. "You'll hear that in the beginning of the grandparenting process," he said. "But grandparenting, like parenting, is a long-term process. That scenario is more likely to happen when the grandchild is very young, under three years old. At that point, you are more helpful to the parent, fulfilling an active grandparenting role such as baby-sitting and helping out. It doesn't take as much involvement or energy.

"But once the grandchildren are five or older, that is a more crucial time to get involved because that's when the kids have an awareness of the grandparent. That's also the time when the boomers start thinking of phasing out their active work life. In your late forties and fifties you're still in the midlife phase. The question to ask yourself is: How much can I accomplish in the remaining time I have left in my work life? Boomers are still going full speed ahead in their work. But that soon will change. As they get into their mid-fifties and as their grandchildren get older, boomers will find opportunities to be involved with them."

Because the average American family is smaller than past generations, boomer grandparents have a greater opportunity to be involved in the individual growth and development of their grandkids, he adds. "The bonds between grandchildren and their boomer grandparents will become much stronger if merely by the fact that boomers don't tend to have a lot of children. With fewer grandkids, the boomers will be much closer to those they do have. Fewer relationships mean each one can be more special. Boomers will invest more time and energy into their grandchildren."

Linda (Mimi) Gray: *"I have a busy life with many interests, but for sheer joy and pleasure none compare to being with my granddaughter."*

Boomers are nothing if not contradictory and a little self-absorbed. We might remain liberal in spirit, but we're slowly, steadily, inexorably growing more conservative in our politics and lifestyles. But that doesn't mean we'll be stuffy old codgers. Quite the contrary; it's just that we will be vocal in trying to make life better for our grandkids. In fact, say the experts, boomers will, if we haven't already, embrace many of the same values that we trashed in our youth.

Let's be honest. The boomer-led social revolution of the sixties really did a number on anyone over thirty—especially grandparents. It relegated the role of our elders to that of outmoded human Edsels. No longer did wisdom equate with experience. "It's what's happening now." "If it feels good do it." "Do your own thing." Huge numbers of boomers rejected the traditional values and principles that had been the guiding force for our grandparents and parents.

It took us a while, but we're rediscovering those ideals. And, yes, many of us do feel a little guilty for having belittled and disowned the beliefs of the very people who gave us the self-assurance and security to be our free-to-be selves. Now we're turning that guilt into action.

Strauss and Howe observe in *New Generations*, "A growing chorus of social critics is noticing a Boom-led 'New Puritanism' in circa-1990 America. Fortyish Americans are beginning to police 'politically correct' behavior, pass 'anti-ugly' zoning ordinances, punish students for 'inappropriately directed laughter,' circulate 'Green Lifestyle' guides and attach 'Green Seals' to products, ban obscene music, promote 'chastity,' and even support novel forms of corporal punishment and boot-camp incarceration that [their parents] would never have imagined—and that Boomers, two decades ago, would have considered fascist."

Members of the me generation "have seen the evil of their ways," says Dr. Perry Buffington. "Liberalism to conservatism has a forty-year swing, and that pendulum is definitely swinging away from liberalism. I think we are going back because we feel our culture is so out of control. We are responsible for it so what is happening now is overcorrection.

"You always return to the familiar. Always. In a crisis situation— and many people believe our society is in a moral crisis—you tend to believe that whatever worked once for you will work again. The kinds of behavior we learned during the Beaver Cleaver era are the same ones boomers want to see for our grandchildren. I wouldn't be surprised if boomers return to the Ozzie and Harriet look again."

Boomers will seek to unite the generations, much like it was before the social revolution, according to Dr. Brazelton. We're finally becoming aware of the longing that we missed when we failed to involve our parents in the lives of our kids, he says. "I think the concept of the extended family was lost in your generation probably because of the generation gap. That was really tragic because that left your generation with nobody to fall back on when you got into trouble. And raising children can be full of trouble. This longing [to involve elders in family life] will push boomers to be better grandparents."

> **Alisa (Nana) Dollar:** *"Grandchildren are bright-eyed, innocent little blessings. It's amazing to see in your own children the extension of your spouse and yourself— and to see it extended yet further through your grandchildren is truly a remarkable happening."*

Grandchildren present boomers with a mulligan—another shot at being there for the family.

"Even though boomers are active and egocentric, we will come to the awareness that maybe we should have invested more in our own children," says Dr. Martin. "But it's too late to do that for them, so maybe we'll have a second chance to do that with our grandchildren."

Dr. Buffington agrees. "Boomers raised hell in the sixties, their kids in the seventies, their blood pressure in the eighties, and their personal deficits in the nineties. Now as grandparents, it's time for redemption. They will get involved with their grandchildren if for no other reason than to undo what they screwed up in their own kids. They get another chance to show their paternal and maternal mettle, not to mention assuaging their guilt. They should make better teachers of morality. Having been there and done that, they'll keep their grandkids from going to those same places and doing those same things.

"Boomers are now dealing with the worry that as parents we were lousy. We see it, to some degree, in how our children turned out and that bothers us. Through grandparenthood, we are now convinced that we have a reprieve, a dispensation from God. We have another chance to help rear children. We see grandparenting as a way to absolve ourselves of guilt from being so job-conscious, so corporate-conscious that the family came second. We may have failed our families in the seventies and eighties, but, by God, we're not going to fail again."

Dr. Martin doesn't think we should beat ourselves up over any perceived parenting faults. "We have done a better job of raising children than people think. Yes, we've had to juggle jobs and family. But we engaged our children in all kinds of activities—soccer, music lessons, and so many other things that we, as children, didn't have the opportunity to do. We'll no doubt want to encourage our grandchildren to be involved in all sorts of activities."

And this could lead to another issue. We're likely to be quite vocal in how our grandchildren are raised, Dr. Martin believes.

The activist side of us "could translate into overly active grandparents more than perhaps their adult children would like."

Though pacifist in nature, we boomers have been raised to question, argue with, and ultimately disobey orders that aren't in sync with our own beliefs. We may be just as assertive with our adult children when it comes to caring for our grandkids.

"When boomers were younger we didn't trust older people, but that won't stop boomer grandparents from wanting to serve in some sort of a consulting mode in the lives of their adult children," says Dr. Martin. "The current grandparenting mode is, 'Ask me, and I'll give you advice.' The boomer grandparents are likely to have the attitude, 'I'll give you advice; take it or leave it.' We won't wait to be asked for advice.

"The baby boom generation has changed the agenda of almost everything in this country—husbands, wives, families. I wouldn't be surprised to see boomer grandparents be a bit too bossy with their adult children [in how the grandchildren are raised] to the extent that the middle generation might get a little upset about it.

"The middle generation typically negotiates between the grandparents and the grandchildren such things as the amount of contact and the quality of the interaction. That might change with the boomer grandparents. They may build their own bridge directly to their grandchildren and disregard the middle generation."

If the experts are right, it's two thumbs up for the boomer grandparents. "I think there is good news," says Dr. Kornhaber. "Today's new grandparents have really started to think about more emotional, spiritual, and family imperatives to life now that they've passed the boundaries of materialism and the me generation. The pendulum is swinging back, and I am seeing a growing consciousness about the importance of the family."

Things from Our Childhood That Our Grandkids Likely Will Never See

Blackjack and Beeman's gum
Powerhouse candy bars
licorice records
wax teeth, lips, mustaches
wax Coke-shaped bottles with colored sugar water
candy lipstick
candy cigarettes
Fizzies
soda pop machines that dispense bottles
pull tabs that snapped off soda cans
tableside jukeboxes in coffee shops
home milk delivery in glass bottles with cardboard stoppers
movies preceded by cartoons and newsreels
party lines
rotary phones
drive-ins with car hops
sock hops
winter rubber boots with metal latches
coonskin hats
P. F. Flyers
angora sweaters
bouffant hairdos
spoolies
hair dryers with plastic caps
flattop haircuts
butch wax
dart guns with rubber-tipped darts
tin-can telephones
peashooters
cork popguns

roll of cap-gun caps
Howdy Doody puppets
Beanie and Cecil dolls
two-bladed ice skates that clip onto shoes
roller skates that clip onto shoes
roller skate keys
S & H Green Stamps and Plaid Stamps
metal lunchboxes
Winky Dink kits for drawing on the TV screen
crystal radios
console hi-fis with 78s
45-rpm records
hand-crank wringers on tub washing machines
slide rules
levered metal ice trays
mimeograph paper
carbon paper
flash bulbs
eight-track tape decks
home movie cameras
Dick and Jane readers

Good Vibrations

The Expectant Grandparent

The Age Thing

One day you pick up the phone and learn you're going to be a grandparent. You're ecstatic (assuming the call is not from your unmarried daughter who's dating a falsetto-voiced Tiny Tim wannabe). You're thrilled. You're jubilant. And at the height of your joy, you reach a sobering conclusion: grand + parent = old.

More of us than might care to admit it probably have encountered a negative feeling or two over becoming a grandparent. But that's natural, say the experts, who add that we shouldn't get mired in guilt or self-recrimination if we experience such contrary emotions. They are most often caused by our fixation on youthfulness or by our inability to be ready psychologically for this role.

The happiness of becoming nanas and papas sometimes gives way to tinges of sadness or even depression because the news forces us to confront the fact that we're no longer as young as we think. Like Arte Johnson's decrepit geezer getting whacked over the head by Ruth Buzzi's little old lady, we're knocked senseless by the reality of aging.

So what if your heart rate is better than it was fifteen years ago or you look and feel sexier than ever (especially after collagen injections and liposuction)? Like it or not, you're motoring down the road of life with brakes that don't work. You've passed the territories of childhood and parenthood and are entering grandparenthood where the neon sign on the roadside diner flashes, "Last Stop Before Senility." Your years are numbered—and they total less than the sum of Beatles hits.

Wasn't it just yesterday you weren't trusting anybody over thirty? Now you don't trust anybody under thirty.

> **Linda (Mimi) Gray:** *"When I got the 'Mom, I'm pregnant' call, the first thing I did after I hung up was rush into the bathroom and look at myself in the mirror, wondering, 'Do I look like a grandmother?'"*

Afraid that grandparenting will make you feel old? Tough, say experts. Your grandkids are going to think you're old no matter what your age—even if you are too young to remember *Hopalong Cassidy* on Saturday morning TV. But it's okay, because kids don't care. "Even though Grandma is running around now in Spandex, the kids see her as someone with age, and that's just fine with them," says psychologist Dr. Perry Buffington. "Kids see grandparents as timeless."

So accept your fate. Grandparenting may not sound sexy in our age-obsessed society, but it definitely has its own cachet—one that boomer nanas and papas should relish.

If your ego is still swirling with mixed emotions over your impending status, you might need a little attitude adjustment. Grasp this: Your child is giving you the gift of a wonderful new human being, part of your living legacy. That's cause for celebration, for you to get psyched. A precious little person is about to enter your life and capture your heart. Joy to the world! If anything, you ought to feel the envy of those friends who're wondering when they'll become grandparents too.

Peggie: *"I am forty-three years old and just found out I will be a grandmother in seven months! I am really struggling with the idea and certainly can't stand the idea of being called Grannie, Grandma, or Nana. . . . What am I to do? . . . I am sure I will get used to the idea, but for now I am in shock and still feel that I am too young to be known as 'Grannie.'"*

If you're fretting over this age thing, put a new spin on your upcoming role. Assuming you're healthy and active and have cleverly hidden your gray hair (you men still have hair, don't you?), you, like the models on the cover of this book, probably don't look your age. So play up the fact that you are, or will be, a grandparent. Don't be shy. Announce it wherever you go—the fitness center, the board meeting, the chiropractor. It'll do you good.

Kathy: *"My mother-in-law and I were at a restaurant talking about my grandchildren, and the waitress couldn't believe I was a grandmother. She thought I looked too young. Man, that sure felt good. I find myself mentioning I'm a grandmother often because I enjoy hearing those 'you-don't-look-like-a-grandma' comments—and I know they won't last forever. God, I wonder how I'll feel when they do stop."*

We need to boot out of our consciousness those lingering childhood perceptions of grandparents as being wrinkled senior citizens. Heck, your parents or grandparents were probably your age—or even younger—when they became nanas and papas. They just looked older to you because you were seeing them through the eyes of a child or young parent.

Sue (Nana) Crawford, fifty-two: *"I don't see myself as an old lady, not like my grandparents. Hmmm.*

> *My grandmother was forty-five when I was born and I always thought she was an old lady. Oh, well, I'm sure my grandkids [both under the age of two] will think the same thing about me because the bag boys at the grocery store think I'm old now."*

You probably look much younger and better than your mom and dad when you made them grandparents, right? They were set in their ways, watching TV in the BarcaLounger, going to Tupperware parties, and playing golf. They weren't like you (okay, except for the golf). They didn't skydive, run 10-Ks, or in-line skate. Did people ever mistake your mom for your sister à la Grandma Naomi Judd and her daughter Wynonna? Could your father hop across the stage like Grandpa Mick Jagger singing "Let's Spend the Night Together"?

We aging boomers are determined to redefine what it means to get older. As TV news personality Linda Ellerbee said recently about turning fifty, "We are a generation that believes we can have it our way, mainly because we so often have. Most of us do not face this age thing gracefully. We fight. Some harder than others. Some of us go into heavy denial.

"We can exercise ourselves to the skin and bone. We can eat nothing but broccoli. We can pay the plastic surgeon, dye our hair, date (and/or marry) much younger men and women . . . quit old careers . . . and change old habits, but we cannot stop time. We cannot go back and be who we were. Those people are gone."

Gone are the flower children, potheads, go-go dancers, grunts, grads, hippies, yippies, and yuppies that we once were. We're grandparents now. And, for some, it's unsettling.

"I had a hard time at first acknowledging that I was going to be a grandmother," admits Susan Ginsberg, Ed.D., editor and publisher of the national newsletter *Work & Family Life.* "It seemed like other people would think I was so old.

"It's not uncommon for you to experience some denial. Grandparenting is not part of your self-image. I know many people became grandparents reluctantly—kicking and screaming because it was an assault on their self-image. But most people get used to it very quickly. When you see friends your age becoming grandparents, then it makes you feel better. There's a whole world of grandparents who look and act young. They work and are busy doing things. But there's still so much focus in society on being young that it's stupid.

"When my granddaughter was seven she told me, 'You're not a real grandma.' 'Why not?' I asked. She said, 'You don't have gray hair, you work, and you go to exercise class. What's wrong with you?' I told her, 'There are lots of different kinds of grandmas and some feel and look younger than others.'"

> **Bob (Boppy) Giavonni:** *"I was really happy with the news of being a grandfather. But, I confess, there was a part of me that said, 'Man, you're getting old!'"*

Our culture works against grandparenthood by focusing on looking forever young, laments grandparenting guru Dr. Arthur Kornhaber. "Grandparenting isn't sexy. According to society, if I'm a grandparent, I'm old. One guy I know wanted his grandsons to call him 'Uncle'; another didn't want to be known as 'Grandpa' because he wouldn't be able to flirt with the secretaries.

"Grandparenting consciousness is not recognized or savored in this country. Grandparenting as a function is equated with old age, and no one wants to be old."

Boomer grandparents need to embrace this next phase of their life, says Dr. Kornhaber. "We have to change our culture so 'old' means you're ennobled, you're powerful, you're important. But our value system is so corrupt, ridiculous, and unrealistic that those traits of aging don't fit."

You must retool your thinking and get pumped up about this new stage of your life and enjoy it, he added. "As you age, you have an enormous opportunity to grow, to become more forgiving, less judgmental, more accepting, and more compassionate. You should talk openly about the importance of elders doing what we've been hardwired to do for all of human existence—nurture and teach the younger generation while the middle generation is working. The consciousness of the importance of the family connection between young and old needs to be raised to a new level.

"I'm hoping the boomer generation will start to understand this and develop a new image of aging in our culture. Hopefully they'll be receptive to this idea because the power of aging can be a pretty sexy idea once you get rid of the notion that old age means playing shuffleboard and watching yourself go down the tubes. Our culture must appreciate the usefulness of elders. Selling that concept will be a really big challenge for the boomer grandparents."

Even if you're hung up on age, your grandchildren won't be. "Children don't have age prejudice," says Dr. Kornhaber. "They don't see a fifty-year-old person. They see a grandparent who they think is wonderful and who they love deeply. Children will tell me what about their grandparent makes them happy, what makes him or her worth something to them, why they adore their grandparent. It has nothing to do with anything physical like how young the grandparent looks. Besides, wrinkles are interesting to kids anyway.

"It's this idea of 'I am how I look and not how people feel about me' that gets boomers into trouble. When you age, there's nothing you can do about things sagging and joints creaking. That's normal. You are going to have to deal with how you view self-worth. It's very important to minimize this kind of physical attraction as a basis for self-esteem. There must be a shift in values."

Are You Ready?

As an expectant or new grandparent, you might have come to grips with the age issue, yet still might not be ready psychologically, Dr. Kornhaber says. "Readiness for grandparenthood depends on attaining an optimum developmental state and having the time, the appropriate psychological and philosophical attitudes, and the appropriate family situation to be a grandparent.

"After raising their children, everyone needs a rest to recenter themselves and their identity. Hopefully they are afforded an opportunity to fulfill some of their own private needs and dreams. Eventually that drive to become a grandparent bubbles up and you're ready to nurture grandchildren. That's the ideal situation."

Some people in Dr. Kornhaber's Grandparent Study said they wanted to wait until they were older before becoming grandparents. Other unready grandparents hoped to pursue their personal goals full-time or had preconceived ideas about the right time in their lives to be grandparents. One woman told him, "I'll be happy to be a grandmother when I'm sixty-five, not now when I'm only fifty-two. I've got some time for myself for the first time in my life. This is 'me' time." A few people in the study were not thrilled about becoming grandparents because they felt overburdened with other caregiving responsibilities.

Bliss, reminds Dr. Kornhaber, is dependent on the emotional happiness of the entire family and those closest to us. "We used to define ourselves by our relationships to our friends and family." Maybe that's what we should bring back into vogue, he says.

> **Anne Bernays (in *Town & Country Monthly*):**
> *"I tried hard to be cool about the looming first grandchild . . . but my unconscious tricked me into misreading the nameplate on a Pontiac as 'Grand Ma' when it was clearly 'Grand Am.'"*

When we learn that we're going to be grandparents, it's common for us to take stock of ourselves and count all the successes, failures, and unfulfilled dreams. You're in your late forties or early fifties, and the truth is you're not going to pilot the space shuttle or throw passes for the Miami Dolphins or cut a record with Jimmy Buffett. You made choices. Now, as you reach the grandparenting stage, you're ready to make more choices. Take this opportunity to rethink your priorities for the remaining years of your life. What is it that's really worth doing? Grandparenting should rank high on the list.

Meanwhile, don't fuss over the strange emotions you might experience over news of your impending new role as a grandparent.

"If you have mixed feelings about becoming a grandparent, relax. They prove you're only being human," says Dr. Buffington. "You don't need to feel ashamed over that angst or anguish. Accept them and even talk about them. Most people usually work through these feelings pretty quickly. The moment you hold that grandchild and bond with that baby, those conflicting feelings should melt away."

Here's what cyber-columnist Pat Connolly wrote (quoted here in edited form, with her permission) when she learned that she was going to be a nana at the age of forty-six:

> "Hi! My name is Pat and I'm a grandmother."
>
> I was sure that this is how I would introduce myself from now on, like a confession at an AA meeting. Or worse yet, I wouldn't have to say anything—everyone would just know by looking.
>
> It was very traumatic the night I found out my daughter was pregnant. As I sat looking at her and her proud husband toasting with a bottle of champagne, all I could see in my mind was a bent, white-haired, wrinkled woman whose total life became dedicated to a small child. Grandmother!

As the weeks turned into months, I noticed whenever the fact came up that I was going to be a grandmother, I had a sense of wonder followed by an upset feeling. How could I let anyone know what was going on inside my head? Everyone thought it was such a good idea. I must be thrilled.

I began to think I wasn't such a great person. I mean, people were saying grandmothers-to-be are coming into a great part of their lives. (I noticed the ones saying this were mostly the white-haired grandmothers.) How come it didn't look that way to me? What's wrong here?

I tried to put myself at ease as I peered intensely into my mirror. "Well, I'll be a very young-looking grandmother and I won't fall all over the kid. I'll enjoy my time with him or her and then go on with my life."

As my daughter grew bigger, I became more concerned about my feelings. I wouldn't volunteer anything about the impending arrival to my friends. When someone asked me a direct question about the pregnancy, I acted like everything was really great with me. I was supposed to be excited and glad, right? I felt like a traitor. I asked myself, "What's wrong with me? Why am I not excited? Does anyone else feel this way?" I couldn't talk to anyone. Who ever heard of a grandmother-to-be who wasn't really excited and who hated the whole idea?

I jotted down every negative thought I had about becoming a grandmother. Then I tried to recall its origin. You know the one about the white-haired grandmothers? That came from meeting my grandmother's friends at her club when I was eight years old. Even bleached blondes looked like white-haired ladies. It was so funny—and revealing—to discover the origin of each thought, especially the one that goes "Grandmothers are not sexy."

When my oldest daughter was born, my aunt called my dad and said, "Sam, do you know what this makes you?" He replied, "Old—and sleeping with a grandmother!"

That stuck with me. When I became an expectant grandmother, I unthinkingly wore old nightgowns and lower-heeled shoes and didn't wear bright-colored clothes or things that appeared too young for me. I began behaving in what I considered to be a more appropriate way for a grandmother. Yuck!

But then I decided to replace those negative thoughts with positive ones like, "Grandmothers have a lot more time to be athletic." "Grandmothers take care of their bodies so they can stay sexy." "Grandmothers have a lot more freedom to do and be what they want."

I began to practice, practice, practice creating new thoughts. The more advanced the pregnancy became, the more adept I became at changing my old way of thinking. As time drew closer to the baby's arrival, I was very happy about becoming a grandmother and looking for ways to make this time fun and exciting.

Party Time

As Three Dog Night so eloquently put it, "Celebrate! Celebrate! Dance to the music!"

Make a big deal out of your impending grandparenthood. Why should the new or expectant parents get all the glory and attention? Host your own party as a festive way to tell your friends about your new role. For that matter, the next time your friends announce they are going to be, or have just become, grandparents, throw a bash for them.

Michelle (Grammy) Davies: *"Our friends are al-ways looking for excuses to have parties, so when we announced we were going to be grandparents, they threw a party for us. Everyone came as a fictional grandparent—you know, like Heidi's grandpa and Grandmama Addams. It was wild."* (How much do you want to bet that everyone came with canes and gray-haired wigs?)

We have wedding showers and baby showers, so why not grand-parent showers? Be a trendsetter and host one for the new or expectant grandparents. Don't necessarily restrict the shower to women. Couples are often invited to other kinds of showers, so this should be no exception.

Forget the gag gifts and go for something practical. After all, how many new or soon-to-be nanas and papas have everything they need for those times when the baby comes for a visit? A trip to the local baby store can overwhelm rookie grandparents with items that they didn't know they needed—and probably didn't even know were on the market.

Some suggested inexpensive items for a shower:

- toys to start a grandparent's collection
- picture frame or album
- safety kit that includes electrical outlet covers and safety latches
- books for the grandchild
- how-to books for the grandparent (like this one!)
- baby shampoo, soap, towels, and washcloths
- child's eating utensils and unbreakable plates
- safety gate
- baby blanket

For big-ticket items that two or more persons could purchase together, consider:

- crib
- high chair
- car seat
- umbrella stroller

Peggy (Granma) Minacci: *"When I was an expectant grandmother, a friend brought over some toys. I said David and Melissa [the parents-to-be] would really appreciate them. She said, 'They're not for the parents. They're for you when your grandchild comes to visit.' It hadn't occurred to me that I'd need things like that at my house."*

Rite of Passage

Besides showers and parties, mark this moment in a more special, poignant way—a personal gesture or ceremony that adds some significance to your upcoming grandparenthood.

Here's where you take the time and effort to reflect on your new role—how you want to fit into your grandchild's life, what she means to you, what you hope to mean to her. This rite of passage is a way to commemorate your love and involvement in the family. It also helps make grandparenting more than an abstract concept and gives you the opportunity to appreciate your life and your loved ones.

You can create a rite in whatever way suits you—a quiet dinner with your mate at a special restaurant to talk about your feelings; a poem, letter, or song written to the newborn child; a visit to the family grave site to contemplate the link between the past and future; the handcrafting of an item (such as a piece of pottery, sculpture, or wood carving) that symbolizes this new status. Whatever you choose to do, the rite will heighten your awareness of becoming a grandparent.

> **Jane (Nana) Trebble:** *"We planted a peach tree to honor our grandson, Jeremy. As the tree grows, so too will Jeremy. I can't wait until we can all eat peaches from his tree. We plan to grow a tree for each of our other grandchildren—assuming we'll have more."*

> **Tom (Grandpa) Andersen:** *"My wife and I sat down and we each wrote a letter to our granddaughter, Sara, shortly after she was born. We told her how much we loved her and what kind of grandparents we promised to be. We sealed our letters and put them in her hope chest. The letters really forced us to contemplate what it means to be a grandparent. It'll be cool to see what she thinks when she reads our letters."*

Time to Cram

If you haven't already, now is a good time for you to brush up on the latest in prenatal care, birthing, postnatal care, and child development. You'll save yourself plenty of aggravation by being on the same page as the expectant parents. By not hitting the books, you risk acting as annoyingly out of touch as your elders were when you started a family.

"Read the books that the parents-to-be are reading so you can speak the same language," suggests Dr. T. Berry Brazelton. "It's important for you to keep up with the changes that are going on in parenting."

We had *Dr. Spock's Baby and Child Care* as our authority when we were young parents. Today's moms and dads are parenting bookworms who have access to thousands of books on the subject, not to mention magazines, videos, audiotapes, CD-ROMs, and Web sites.

You need to know what's in their heads so you'll at least have some understanding about their decisions (not that there's much you can do if you disagree with them—but more about that in a later chapter). Boy, are there decisions for them to make: Will your grandchild make her grand entrance in a hospital, in a birthing center, or at home? In a tub or a bed? With an obstetrician or a certified nurse-midwife? Will the mother manage pain with analgesic drugs (morphine is out), patient-controlled analgesia, epidural anesthesia, self-hypnosis, or bite-the-bullet willpower? Will the baby be breast-fed or bottle-fed?

By reading what the parents-to-be are reading, you'll get a degree of grandparent comfort in learning the rationale behind their choices. And, who knows, you might learn something.

Today's parents deal with a whole new slate of products, from Boppys to Snuglis to Nuks. Thermometers are placed in babies' ears, under armpits, or on foreheads. Teddy bears play soothing womb sounds while voice-activated cribs begin rocking at babies' first cries.

Have you heard about Lamaze, Bradley, Read, and Gamper? No, it's not a cover band for Crosby, Stills, Nash, and Young. Actually, they're names of popular childbirth methods. If you'd like to know more about what goes on in childbirth classes, ask your son or daughter if you can sit in on a session or two. Most instructors will welcome grandparents. Many hospitals and birthing centers offer special classes for grandparents-to-be, so call around—including the pediatrician's or obstetrician's office—for classes nearest you.

Oh, yeah, there's one more important thing you should do before the baby arrives. Sit down with your adult children and have an honest heart-to-heart. Discuss the role you're going to play as a grandparent.

I've Got to Be Me

Defining Your Grandparenting Role

The Big Gig

What kind of nana or papa will you be? The formal elder who shows interest and concern in the grandkids but adopts a hands-off policy? The informal fun-seeker who enjoys getting down and dirty with the grandkids? The surrogate who cares for the grandkids while the parents are working or absent? The distant figure who emerges from the shadows on birthdays, holidays, and special occasions?

Give it some serious thought, because you're going to be a grandparent for the rest of your life. In fact, you'll likely be one for more than half your adult life, not only because you're still relatively young but because you should live much longer than previous grandparents did.

This is no lame honorary position granted you simply because you have a child who's had a child. Your role is much more crucial and vital to the family than you think. Don't take our word for it. Listen to what the experts have to say:

- Dr. T. Berry Brazelton, nationally recognized pediatrician: "I think grandparents are more important than they ever were. With both parents working and the divorce rate rising, it's really critical for the grandparents to be there as a steady beacon for their grandchildren."

- Dr. Perry Buffington, psychologist and syndicated columnist: "How important is being a grandparent today? More than you can possibly imagine! I say that with an exclamation point."

- Dr. Arthur Kornhaber, founder of the Foundation for Grandparenting: "I'm saying you count and you can change things for the better. Grandparents are terribly, terribly important to their families, especially to their grandchildren."

Research supports their views. The grandparent-grandchild bond is second in emotional importance only to that of the parent-child bond, according to the Grandparent Study. In confirming that grandparents and grandchildren deeply affect each other's lives, the study found that children who enjoy close relationships with at least one grandparent:

- feel accepted "as is" and even "adored"
- are more emotionally secure than those who have no such ties
- gain comfort in knowing they have a place to go—an "emotional sanctuary"—in times of trouble
- extend their love for their grandparents to all older people, have a positive image of aging, and are less likely to be ageist
- show greater respect for parents in households that foster the grandparent-grandchild relationship
- have an enriched understanding of the world because of what their grandparents teach them about earlier times and ways of living
- feel rooted in the past and enjoy a sense of belonging to a "family ego"

According to Native American beliefs, when you are grand-parenting, you are nurturing not just your own grandchildren but seven generations yet unborn. You are making a difference in the lives of your grandkids and enjoying their personalities, and at the same time the rewards of your grandparenting extend well into the future.

Most new grandparents today have little idea what a lasting, positive impact they can make in the lives of their grandchildren. What will your grandkids say about you fifteen to twenty years from now? Perhaps they will echo the responses of college students who took part in a recent study by Dr. Gregory Sanders and Debra Trygstad of North Dakota State University.

The researchers found that 81 percent of the students described their relationship with the grandparent they saw most often as "extremely important." The majority said their grandparent kept them informed of family heritage (83.6 percent), gave them money (69.6 percent), provided emotional support (66.7 percent), and offered personal advice (63.4 percent). Their love for their grand-parent didn't diminish as both grew older. Although 71.5 percent of the students saw their grandparent no more than monthly, 81 percent said this amount of contact was less than they desired.

"The love between a grandparent and grandchild is uncondi-tional," says Dr. Kornhaber. "It's the simplest and least compli-cated intense human love bond. It's 'I love you because you exist.' Jean-Paul Sartre said he could make his grandmother go into raptures of joy just by being hungry. This unconditional love is in-credibly empowering for children.

"If grandparents did not exist, children surely would invent them. Children feel a natural connection between themselves and their grandparents. They exhibit a strong emotional need for close attachment to at least one grandparent. When they see each other, they get very happy and light up."

You've been freed from all the duties and constraints of a parent, so you can now savor the role of a grandparent. Dr. Brazelton is fond of saying, "Grandparents show children the mountaintops, while parents must teach them the drudgeries of how to get there."

Creating Your Role

While you await the birth of your grandchild, try to figure out what your individual grandparenting role is. What part do you want to play? Keep in mind that your part is not scripted for you, so you get to make up your own role—one that fits your particular lifestyle yet still addresses your grandparenting goals.

To help you get started, ask yourself the following questions:

- How much time can I give my grandchild?
- How involved do I want to be in his life as an infant, a toddler, a preschooler?
- How much does his family need me to handle such chores as baby-sitting or running errands?
- How much am I willing to alter my life at home and work to be with my grandchild?
- What kind of relationship do I want to have with him?
- How can I become someone special in his life?
- What are my needs?
- What image do I want to portray?
- How do I want to be remembered?

There are no right or wrong answers. Every nana and papa is different; every situation unique. For a little inspiration, look at the traits that you've admired in other grandparents. Just remember that you can't shape your role adequately if you feel obligated to match an unrealistic image of your grandparents, thereby feeling guilty if you fail. Figure out what qualities they had that you want to emulate. But create your own identity.

Kathy: *"After I received the news from Allison that I was going to be a nana, my reaction of 'Wow, this is great!' turned into, 'Oh my God. Now what do I do? What kind of a grandmother do I want to be? Can I, should I, be like Grandma Lang?'*

"My grandmother was wonderful. She was a large woman who lived on a farm and could do just about everything. She patiently taught me to cook, knit, quilt, sew, and garden.

"After Allison's call I wondered, 'Am I going to have to do all those things for my grandchildren? I don't like baking cookies. Sewing? Knitting? It's cheaper to buy clothes. And I never was very good at those things anyway.'

"But then I realized a grandmother's love and attraction to her grandchild is as natural and deep as the love she felt toward her own babies. Some ways of showing that love will always remain the same. But as times change, so do grandparenting styles.

"So I don't bake cookies. I love to travel. What fun it will be to take the grandchildren to the Keys, Manhattan, and Disney World. We'll introduce them to our interests like archaeology, photography, and canoeing. We'll outfit them with backpacks and hike along the Appalachian Trail, climb rocks on the Blue Ridge Mountains, and raft down the Nantahala.

"But maybe I'll make cookies after all. For some reason, cookies and grandmothers still seem to go together."

"The basic role of the grandparent hasn't changed at all—it's the unqualified love and support of your adult children and your grandchildren," says noted educator Barbara Bowman, president of the Erikson Institute. "And that doesn't change no matter what other stresses and strains there are in life."

If you want to be the most effective grandparent possible, she says, you must offer emotional, spiritual, physical, and financial support to your grandchild's family.

"With mothers in the workforce and the decrease in men's real wages, the strain on families is greater now," says Bowman. "And when you throw in divorce, family life is more stressful than it was a generation ago. Young families need more support and help from grandparents than the previous generation did. They need someone to baby-sit, to pick up diapers, to sometimes give them money. It's more than just being nice. It's being helpful."

The two biggest factors in determining the roles and involvement you'll play as a grandparent in a stable family are your time and your relationship with the young parents.

> **Sue (Nana) Crawford:** *"I'm real bad about saying no when it comes to baby-sitting. I don't speak up. There isn't any real reason why I can't. Just because I don't want to [baby-sit] doesn't seem like a good enough reason."*

You should talk things out with the new parents—the sooner the better—and try to fashion an understanding, says Bowman. "One grandparent might say, 'I can sit one day a week,' another will say, 'Whenever you need me, call me.' It depends on your relationship with your kids. Most parents know their children pretty well by the time they start having babies of their own. As a general rule, the more specific grandparents and parents can be about roles, the better."

But be diplomatic and respectful when talking with the young parents, says Dr. Buffington. "If you come right out during the pregnancy and say, 'This is what I will do and won't do,' without really discussing things, it won't work. Hormones are coursing through their veins and they'll take it as a direct affront. Explain in what ways you can help them and then tell them your time limitations in a very positive fashion."

> **Nana Jo:** *"My daughter got her self-esteem from her job. I hear things like, 'I didn't go to college to change diapers.' Child-rearing is unfulfilling to her in some ways so I don't think she'll be a stay-at-home mom for much longer. I do some things for her that I don't really want to do just to take the pressure off of her so she'll stay home longer with the children."*

Says Susan Ginsberg, Ed.D., editor and publisher of the national newsletter *Work & Family Life*, "To make grandparenting work, you have to set parameters and have some realistic expectations on both sides. Like many boomer grandparents, you probably have obligations other than work and family. Tell your adult child: 'I will do what I can' and then make sure you follow through.

"So much has to do with the way your adult children respond to you. What is their expectation of you? Are they going to lay the guilt on you and put you in positions where you have to say no to them because you are working? Boomers are not the stereotypical grandparents of old who have lots of time on their hands. That's what your children have to get used to. You have a life."

> **Linda (Mimi) Gray:** *"I'm more than just a grandmother. I am a wife, a mother, a businesswoman, a church worker, a volunteer, a tennis player. I love my kids and grandchild dearly, but I have a life of my own to lead."*

Whatever grandparenting roles you choose, be true to yourself and respect your needs. Don't feel guilty if they don't match up to the expectations of others, says Dr. Buffington. "The best, age-old, trite advice in the world is to approach it [differences with your adult children over your role] as honestly as you can. Be as straight as you can and compromise the best that you can. If you do, you have no reason to be afraid or ashamed for taking charge of your life."

> **Keri (Grams) Lytle:** *"My grandmother said things like, 'No matter what you say or do, make sure your kids smell nice,' and 'Don't let the kids go barefoot until after the first of May.' I hope my grandchildren don't expect me to come up with sayings like that."*

In her book *Innovative Grandparenting,* author and grandmother Karen O'Connor writes:

> We can be who we are right now. Stereotypes are out. Individuals are in. You can be who you are and still be a "great" grandmother or grandfather—whether you live in a trailer or a tent, in a condo or a cottage, in a hotel or a house.
>
> The important things haven't changed, namely the presence of a grandparent in the life of a child, your presence in the life of your grandchildren.
>
> If we are to avoid the stereotypes and enjoy our grandparenting years without guilt and without the imposition of others' standards, it will be important to know who we are and who we are not, what we are willing to do and what we are unwilling to do.
>
> I feel certain of one thing. It's okay, in fact it's important and necessary, for each of us to have a life apart from grandparenting. We need definition and purpose beyond our role in the life of our children and grandchildren. We were on earth before them, and they are likely to be here long after we're gone, so it's not healthy to cling to them for our identity.

Doing the Hustle

Dealing with full-time work, outside activities, and personal needs while still maintaining a close relationship with your grandchild can turn your life into a twenty-four-hour-a-day Latin hustle.

"When my daughter gave birth in Boston, I raced up from New York to see her in the hospital and then I had to race back to New York because I had to make a presentation at a conference," Dr. Ginsberg recalls. "I'm not as available as I'd like. I don't have the flexibility of the grandmother who doesn't work. I admit I have grandmother guilt. I'm aware you shouldn't feel guilty about things you can't control. That's good advice but not always effective.

"Sometimes it depends on the kind of support your adult child has. In my case, I have a daughter whose mother-in-law doesn't work. She's there, she's available, and she's wonderful. That takes the onus off of me a little bit.

"You need to set priorities and manage your time. For example, there is a Grandparents' Day at my granddaughter's school. There would have to be a very serious business obligation to keep me away. That's a priority. I go and I love it."

Your grandparenting role will be as important to you as the time you are willing to spend on it, says Bowman. "It's a choice a grandparent has to make. If you aren't willing to baby-sit your grandchild or have him over for the weekend, you're not going to have the same level of intimacy with him that you'll have if you get to put him to bed occasionally."

In her own family, the grandparents still work. "But we're at the stage in our careers where we're more flexible in our work time. I have less and less concern about taking time out to do things with my granddaughter."

Nana on the Net: *"When I'm going to have my beautiful granddaughter Jenna, I make sure my schedule is*

> *clear. No work, no appointments, no chores. I clear*
> *my day to give her total 'grandma' time."*

Dr. Buffington believes there are many boomer grandparents who can juggle their work, volunteer efforts, and other activities and still be good nanas and papas. That's usually because they already have figured out their roles.

He adds, "Ideally, we should create in our minds a mission statement: 'This is what I will do in my life.' Then set priorities. Look at the things you enjoy and ask yourself which you like more—golf, bridge, whatever, or spending time with your grandkids. Then make the appropriate decision. Do you have to spend extra time at work that keeps you away from your grandkids? Sometimes your financial situation gives you no choice. You have to work. That's the nature of the beast and you shouldn't feel guilty about it. That's just the way it is. You need to really examine your life."

Dr. Kornhaber believes in maintaining a balance between your personal life, your work, and family responsibilities: "Many families are reexamining their priorities, and grandparents are seeking to balance their lives more effectively," he said. "Grandfathers today are beginning to understand that their role affords them an opportunity to be with children—something that this new generation of grandfathers had little time for in their younger days.

"I've often taken a day off from my practice and spent it with the grandkids. This is what I mean by balance. A lot of us have jobs that allow us to do that. I'm going to balance my life because the babies are so cute for the first several years. I want to be there because the babies go crazy when they see their grandparents. I want to savor that time in life. That's where the concept of balance comes in. I don't have to be a sixty-hour-per-week work drone. I can pull back a little. I want to spend a little more time with the grandchildren and give the parents a break too."

Changing Roles

Your grandparenting role will evolve as your life and the needs of your family change.

"Do the best you can," suggests Bowman. "If you keep working at it, it gets better. There are times when the needs and demands of the grandchildren conflict with those of the grandparents, and there's no easy way to get around that except through family discussion.

"The best piece of advice I can give is have the adult child be willing to be a parent. It works best when your child carries out the parenting role well and leaves you free to figure out the grandparenting role. When the parenting role isn't being well implemented, it makes it very difficult to be the kind of grandparent you want to be."

An increasing number of boomer nanas and papas are involved in the daily care of their grandchildren from day one—not necessarily by choice but by necessity (a subject discussed in more detail later).

"As the family structure changes, boomer grandparents need to adapt," says Dr. Buffington. "We are seeing more grandparents involved in helping to raise the kids because there are so many single parents who work. The grandparent, usually the grandmother, takes care of the kid during the day because she's cheaper and more trustworthy than other forms of day care. But that's a two-edged sword. You are a parent by day and a grandparent by night. For many, the grandparenting role is evolving into a direct parenting role, which could cause problems in the long run. They are acting more like parents than grandparents.

"But you must be there for your family. You give them a safety net of stability in times of crisis. Sometimes you just need to lend a hand. That's what families do."

If you weren't around as much as you should have been when

your kids were growing up, having your first grandchild can spur you to become a new person. Maybe you were getting Vinnie Barbarino grades in parenting. Well, here's your opportunity to transform yourself and change your family's perception of you. "When you become a grandparent, you can reinvent yourself," says Dr. Buffington. "You can absolve yourself of all your failures as a parent and start all over when you're with your grandkids."

Many of us change without making a conscious effort to do so, he says. "There is something neat about male and female roles as you age. Many of us fit stereotypical feminine and masculine roles until we hit about fifty and then those roles reverse. Where women were more emotional, they become more analytical, and men become more emotional and nurturing. That's why you see this hard-hitting CEO who, when he becomes fifty, turns into a doting grandfather. He doesn't know it, but God just paid a cheap hormonal trick on him.

"As you age, you become more other-centered rather than self-centered. It's wonderful. Especially if you have achieved what you want in life and if you are where you want to be. Grandparenting is like a swan song. It's your last official family role. It's your gift to the world."

The Role of Great-Grandparents

The boomer generation is also the sandwich generation. We're the first to see, in large-scale numbers, our parents become great-grandparents. Because of medical advances and healthier living, the fastest-growing segment of the U.S. population is those people over the age of eighty-five. In fact, it's estimated that half of today's grandparents will eventually become great-grandparents.

So where do the great-grandparents fit in the family picture?

"It depends on their vitality," says Dr. Kornhaber. "If great-grandparents are still somewhat active and in good health, then they become the number-one icon in their family. They don't necessarily have the role as nurturers but they can certainly function as living ancestors and family historians. They can give children firsthand accounts of life in another time. They are the family archivists, providing grandchildren with a link to the past through stories of relatives long dead."

Great-grandparents are living symbols who provide a sense of family roots and give children a new perspective for understanding the past, present, and future.

"Involve the great-grandparents as long as you can," urges Dr. Buffington. "They are a joy from heaven." When a child talks to his great-grandparents, he can connect with as many as six generations—his own, his parents', his grandparents', and his great-grandparents', and through their firsthand accounts his great-great- and great-great-great-grandparents'.

"The great-grandparent serves as the trunk of the family tree," says North Dakota State professor Dr. Gregory Sanders. "It's a living trunk, and all those branches are tied together by that person. We usually don't think about establishing relationships with distant cousins, but when you have that living connection, there's more pride in the family and more of an opportunity to get together and make connections. There are cousins and second cousins twice removed who would not normally be gathering together if they hadn't had a connection with that elderly person."

If you haven't already, get your parents or other elderly relatives in front of a video camera and start pumping them for family stories and anecdotes before it's too late. For that matter, plop yourself down in front of the camera and start reminiscing about your childhood, like the time you threw up on Mr. Wizard's TV show or got a ride in the Weinermobile.

But grandparents whose parents are still living often face a dilemma. "If we don't already, we'll have multiple caregiving roles," says Dr. Peter Martin of Iowa State University. "You are involved in your adult children's and grandchildren's lives as well as your parents'. Who is going to provide for your parents' needs? Where are they going to live? When are you going to visit them? Are you going to have the time and money to fly to Kansas City to see the grandkids and then go on to Arizona to visit your parents?"

> **Sue (Nana) Crawford:** *"I'm part of the sandwich generation so I spend a lot of time helping my mother and [Sue's daughter] Chrisy with the two kids. I don't have time for me. When I go to our beach house, that's my escape. When I'm gone, they fend for themselves because they can do it. I still feel that sense of responsibility to Chrisy to try and make things easier because she's still my kid."*

Adds Dr. Susan Ginsberg, "When you have older parents, more crises come up quickly that you must respond to. It can be hard, especially if your children or grandchildren need you. That's when you must get other relatives to share the responsibility. You can't be expected to take care of four generations by yourself."

> **Sherry (Grammy) Johnson:** *"The grandkids help me sometimes with their great-grandparents. It's a life struggle-juggle."*

The First Time
Ever I Saw Your Face

The New Grandparent

To Be (There), or Not to Be (There)

Allan: *"I was blown away when I held Chad for the first time. I don't know if I was shell-shocked from realizing I was now a grandfather or from realizing that my first-born was now a mother."*

Michelle (Granny) Davies: *"When I first saw my grandson, I thought, 'Oh, goody, I finally have someone I can spoil rotten.'"*

Keri (Grams) Lytle: *"I will never forget the feeling I had holding [granddaughter] Maddie just minutes after her birth. It was indescribable joy and wonder. I bawled almost as loudly as she did."*

Where will you be (or where were you) at the birth of your grand-child? In the waiting room? In the birthing room? At home or at work waiting for the phone call? (We're not talking about the boomers whose grandchildren were born in the bathroom of a 747, in a crowded subway, next to the dairy case of a convenience store, or at the wedding altar—all of which really happened.)

Whether or not it's your first grandchild, to fully appreciate this most profound of experiences, you really need to be there at the birth, says Dr. Arthur Kornhaber. "The new mother and father are giving their parents a gift of a child. It's very important that the grandparents are there to receive that gift."

Boomer dads were the first fathers on a large scale to gain admittance into the delivery room beginning in the seventies. Now our generation is banging on the door to let family and friends share in the blessed event. Today an increasing number of boomer nanas and papas are attending the birth of their grandchild or are standing right outside the door during the delivery.

"The birth of a new family member is a momentous experience," says Dr. Kornhaber. "The happiness, fulfillment, and spiritual joy that every baby brings reaches far beyond the mother and father to resonate within the hearts of all family members.

"When I delivered babies, I had grandmothers come into the room. It's the most incredible experience. It's so powerful the room lights up. You remember in the movie when Charlton Heston, as Moses, went up the mountain and came down with white hair? That's what it's like."

> **Charles Hersch:** *"We waited anxiously [outside the delivery room]. And then we heard the sound—the baby's first cry, surely one of the most thrilling and profound experiences of my life. It truly stands alone, and I am so grateful for having been there. The baby was brought out and passed around. While that was wonderful, it did not equal the shock of that first sound, the sudden realization that our grandchild was really here. If you have the opportunity to experience what we did, I would enthusiastically urge you to seize it."*

Peggy (Granma) Minacci: *"There were fourteen of us standing right outside the delivery room. Right after Michael Thomas was born, my son David came out. He walked through the crowd with this big smile and everyone parted so he could get to my husband Ken and hug him. It was such a moving experience. The family calls it 'The Happening.'"*

Jane (Grandmom) Whitfield: *"My daughter-in-law Chollet involved her mother, stepmother, and me throughout her pregnancy. We were there [for the sonogram] when she discovered she was going to have a boy. We were all tickled. For the birth, a whole batch of us were outside the delivery room in the hall. It was three A.M. when we heard the baby cry. About a half hour later, we all paraded in. Chollet's mother got to hold the baby first, then me, then her stepmother. It sort of went in a pecking order."*

Not everyone thinks grandparents should be attending the birth. "Watch the video," says Dr. Perry Buffington. "Give the parents their space because the birth is a pretty intimate act. It gives the husband and wife a chance to rebond with each other and with the baby. Doctors and nurses should get out of the way as soon as possible because it's such a personal thing. Only so many people can cut that cord anyway."

Dr. Kornhaber's Foundation for Grandparenting has been championing the cause of nanas and papas attending the birth of their grandchildren. "However," he admits, "we still find a great deal of reluctance on the part of many families to do this. Many reasons are given. One young mother wanted only her husband with her in the delivery room. A grandmother-to-be said, 'I know my daughter-in-law would rather be with her own mother at a time like this.' A nurse told us, 'I can't have the whole family in the delivery room. It isn't sanitary.' One grandfather complained, 'I can't leave work.' These arguments, plausible as they be, miss the point. Of course people are modest, families are different, and everyone's busy. Indeed, hospital policy may work against our good intentions.

"However, no one is saying that Grandma and Grandpa have to be looking over the doctor's shoulder when the baby comes. Grandma, for example, could be in the delivery room and Grandpa outside the door until the delivery is over. Then he could hold the baby, say hello, and place the first teddy bear in the baby's arms. The point is that grandparents should be there to welcome the baby, thank the new parents for the gift of the child, and offer to help in any way necessary—and most of all to share the joy."

Dr. T. Berry Brazelton believes the decision to include the grandparents should be left solely up to the new parents. "I don't see any problem with my being there, but my children might. It's such an individual choice. The birth is a time for enhancing the self-image of the young parents. Personally I think it would be wonderful if all three generations were celebrating in the event. This is how they did it with the Mayans. Everybody participated, everybody groaned when the mother had a labor pain."

> **Carrie (Maw Maw) Dulcette:** *"My daughter Shannon had an at-home birth in a tub attended by a midwife. Shannon invited her family and friends over for the delivery. We had a party in the living room and people wandered in and out, checking on Shannon. As soon as the baby was born, we popped champagne and toasted my grandson Sean."*

We weren't able to be there for the birth of our first grandchild, Chad. So when our daughter Allison was pregnant with our second grandchild, Danny, we asked her if we could be in the delivery room for his birth. But she turned us down.

"I want it to be just Dan [her husband] and me," she explained. "I'd like you right outside the delivery room so you can hear what's going on. Then ten minutes later, after the baby and I are cleaned up, you can come in. Those ten minutes will make up precious bonding time between me, Dan, and the baby. It's such a personal thing between a husband and wife—and I want to keep it that way."

We were at the hospital when Allison was about to give birth to Danny. In fact, we were allowed in the delivery room during labor. We had hoped that everyone would be so preoccupied they would forget about our presence. But then we learned the true meaning of the phrase "when push comes to shove." When Allison began to push, the nurse began to shove us out.

We stood outside, each pressing an ear against the door, straining to hear every word and sound in the delivery room. Next time, we'll each bring a stethoscope or at least a drinking glass to help us hear through the door.

> **Allan:** *"When we heard the baby's first wails, tears of happiness trickled down our faces. Here was a new precious gift of life; a new member of our family to love; a new cherished grandson. Then we broke out laughing because Danny's initial cries sounded like frantic quacks. 'My God,' gasped Kathy, 'Allison gave birth to a duck!'*
>
> *"Dan, the proud dad, came out to announce that mother and baby were doing great. Moments later, we introduced ourselves to Danny, who was no longer quacking and seemed quite content with his new surroundings.*
>
> *"Once Kathy—a.k.a. 'the baby hog'—entered the room, Allison and Dan didn't get to hold Danny very*

much. I have a feeling that if Kathy had been there for
the actual delivery, she would have grabbed the baby
right out of the doctor's arms before the umbilical cord
was even cut."

Kathy: "Even though I wish I had witnessed the births
of each of my grandchildren, I wouldn't have wanted
my parents with me when I delivered our daughters.
Giving birth is an emotional and physical experience
that you can't fully describe unless you've been through
it. You never forget it, even when you start those midlife memory lapses. I never felt closer to each of my
babies or my husband than I did at those times. They
were such deep, wonderful, intimate minutes shared
by mom, dad, and baby and no one else—a moment in
time to be cherished and savored by only the three of us.

"So I understand Allison's decision. Although I'd
still jump at the chance to be in the delivery room, I'm
okay with being outside the door. This is a time for the
three of them. This is not a time for Nana. There will
be plenty of Nana times. Who knows? Maybe when
our other daughter, Sasha, gets pregnant, she'll want
me in the delivery room. If so, I'll be there in a flash."

Allison's friends reported a wide range of experiences about
having grandparents attend a birth. Recalls Allison:

"Kayce had her parents in there. Her mom and dad each held
one of her legs while her husband held her hand. She wouldn't
have it any other way. She loved having her mom and dad in there.

"It was different for Mitzi and for Amy. In both cases, their
parents were with them until the contractions started getting bad,
then they wanted the parents out of there. The parents got upset
seeing their kids in pain and that made Mitzi and Amy more nervous and uncomfortable.

"Regan had her husband and mom in there with her. Regan loved it and her mom did too because her mom had been knocked out when Regan was born. But this time her mom finally got to see a birth, and it was a glorious experience for her.

"Another friend wanted to have her parents with her, but she felt uncomfortable having her in-laws in there. She knew that would be a big problem, so she decided against having any of them with her for the birth.

"Then there was Fran. She had eleven people in the delivery room for her second baby. They were all in the room during labor, and when it came time for her to push they said, 'We'll get out.' She said, 'If you all want to stay, you can. I've had an epidural and I feel great!' She was covered up. So she had her mom, in-laws, and friends—all women—there, and they loved it. All she asked was that there be no pictures taken of her until she had a chance to put on makeup five minutes after the birth. She looked absolutely beautiful in the photos."

Home or Away?

When Allison gave birth to Chad, we headed to their home in Tallahassee. We couldn't wait to see and hold our first grandchild. During the eight-hour drive, we had visions of entering a happy house where two beaming young parents would be cooing at their new son; the rooms would be brimming with festive balloons, flowers, and cards; and we would be spending idle, contented hours admiring the newest member of the family. Yeah, right, and Nixon was blameless for Watergate.

> **Kathy:** *"I walked into the house and immediately grabbed for the baby while practically ignoring my daughter who had just gone through a tremendous emotional and physical experience. She was suffering*

from postpartum blues, excessive bleeding, and engorge-
ment. She was in pain and exhausted. The baby was
crying, and our son-in-law Dan felt helpless and stressed
out. Meanwhile, I was concentrating all my love and
attention on the baby.

"But then it dawned on me that Allison needed
mothering more than Chad needed grandmothering at
this point. I changed the focus of my visit and began
taking care of Allison. I tended to her needs and those
of her family—preparing meals, doing the laundry and
ironing, and cleaning the house. It was hard for me to
watch the new parents struggling through those post-
pregnancy problems. Fortunately, within a couple of
days, everything had worked out. It was still hard for
me, though. I am a 'baby hog' by nature, but I had to
stand back and let the baby and his parents get better
acquainted. Chad belonged to Allison and Dan—and
they had first dibs."

Should you stay at the new parents' house right after the birth
of your grandchild? It depends. If you're going there solely to see
the baby and be entertained, get a hotel room. If you plan on helping out in any way you can, maybe you should remain with them.
But it's up to the new parents.

Dr. Brazleton says he and his wife never stayed in the home of
their adult children right after a birth. "I thought that was intrusive. We stayed in a nearby hotel. We'd go over during the day
and do whatever we could to help out. My wife did all the house-
work. What surprised me was how much our children needed our
physical help.

"As a grandparent, you should support the new parents as much
as they will let you. It's a very vulnerable time, and if you are there
offering advice and intruding, it could really upset the applecart.

You have to be extra respectful of the stress that parents are under. To be available without being intrusive is a very important role for new grandparents."

> **Lisa O'Cain:** *"My daughter asked us to wait for two weeks before flying to Chicago to see them. They wanted to be totally alone. Do you know how hard that was for me? I was worried sick about her and I was way too impatient to see my first grandchild—and there was nothing I could do about it."*

> **Jane (Grandmom) Whitfield:** *"[Her son] Mark and [daughter-in-law] Chollet didn't want anybody there because they wanted to handle things by themselves. No one spent the night with them, but I did bring over meals. The little rascal didn't sleep at all, and Chollet was just worn out. She was at the point where she wasn't sure this motherhood was all that great. I remember how worn out I was when I was a new mother. I called Chollet and said, 'If there's anything I can do, I'll be there in a minute.' But they managed to handle it on their own."*

> **Sue (Nana) Crawford:** *"I flew up right after the baby was born and stayed with them. I slept on the living room sofa for five nights and went to the grocery store and cooked. [Her daughter] Chrisy wanted me there yesterday because she was having a difficult time at first. I wish I had arrived before the baby was born."*

Taking a small informal poll of new mothers, we found that virtually all said they wanted and needed help during the baby's first few days at home. They suggested that grandparents can make life easier during this time by:

- Not voicing your opinions, unless asked, about the choice of the baby's name.
- Respecting the new mother's need to bond with her child.
- Accepting, without comment, the parents' wishes to follow their methods of baby care even if they're different than what you followed as a young parent.
- Being sensitive, supportive, and understanding of the new parents.
- Asking what you can do to help—and then doing it, such as doing chores and running errands.
- Bringing over food that requires little or no preparation and is easy to clean up.
- Offering to look after any other children in the family for a few hours (or possibly a few days).
- Getting along with the other grandparents and not competing with them for attention.

If possible, try to fashion an understanding with the young couple before the birth about your immediate role. That way, everyone in the family will know his or her responsibilities and expectations when the baby comes home.

Here's what several new mothers had to say about having the grandparents around:

> **Dana:** *"The grandparents should focus on the needs of the new mom. My mother charged right in, fawned all over the baby, and it was like, 'Hello . . . I'm the mother.' I started to resent it because my baby needed to bond with me. Grandma has the rest of her life to smother him."*

> **Bekka:** *"It was a little too much having relatives there because I was an emotional and physical wreck and I*

felt I had to entertain them. I just wanted Mom and Dad to cook for me and take care of the house and do my dirty work. I didn't want my relatives to see me that way. If they had come a week later, it would have been better."

Stephanie: *"For the first baby, you definitely need someone to stay with you—your mom, a sister, a good friend, whoever you feel close to. For the second baby, I'd love for someone to come a month before and a month after."*

Anna: *"Most of my friends wanted their mothers because they felt more comfortable with them. Some friends didn't want their fathers there because they didn't want their daddies to see them in that kind of state. Moms are used to it, some dads aren't."*

For the birth of your son's or daughter's second child, the focus of your visit should be on caring for the first grandchild. There will be plenty for you to do without being in the way. Typically, the parents are more confident and relaxed and know what to expect during the first few days home with the second child, so you can focus more on your first grandchild.

When you arrive, bring a special gift just for him. Make him the center of attention and keep him entertained, allowing Mom to concentrate on caring for the baby. Spend as much time as possible with the first grandchild, even if it means getting up early to quietly fix breakfast for him and the rest of the family so Mom can sleep between feedings.

Kathy: *"Because Allan and I have flexible schedules, we arrived at Allison's and Dan's home a week before Danny's birth. I'm glad we did because we were able* *to run errands and do chores so that Allison, who was very tired and very uncomfortable, could get some rest.*

"We were better able to chase after Chad, who was almost two years old at the time, and play with him. It took us a couple of days to get down his routine—including play group, nap time, bath time, and bedtime. We also had time to learn 'Chad-speak.' (We finally figured out that 'Ah do' means 'All done.') By the time Allison went into the hospital to give birth, she was well-rested and had a smooth delivery. And we were getting along great with Chad.

"When Allison returned home with Danny, we made the arrival a fun time for Chad. When he wasn't holding and kissing his little brother, he was spending hours with his nana and papa blowing bubbles, reading books, making sidewalk chalk drawings, playing in the sandbox, and frolicking with the hose. He had such a good time that he didn't show any jealousy or competition for his mother's affection.

"To put it simply: If a two-year-old is happy, everyone is happy."

The best way to help the family, Dr. Brazelton contends, is to fall in love with the baby. "I always say every baby needs at least one person, preferably two, who are passionately in love with him or her. When it gets to be two or more, isn't that baby even luckier?"

They Don't Do It That Way Anymore

Boomer offspring prepare for parenthood as if they are going for their master's degree. They huddle with pediatricians, obstetricians, lactation consultants, midwives, labor and delivery nurses, and birthing coaches. Never mind how many children *you* raised;

in their eyes, you probably know as much about today's baby-care trends as Ralph Kramden knew about personal conflict resolution. Baby care is different now.

That Was Then: As young parents, we put our babies on their stomachs at night.

This Is Now: Medical experts agree that babies should sleep on their backs or sides to lessen the risk of Sudden Infant Death Syndrome.

That Was Then: When we were young parents, our doctors encouraged us to follow a schedule of feedings for our babies.

This Is Now: Today, physicians realize such schedules aren't practical or necessary because babies' hunger varies depending on activity and growth. Babies have a natural hunger drive. They know when they are hungry and when they are full.

That Was Then: When we were young parents, it was common practice to give babies solid food within four to six weeks after birth.

This Is Now: Most experts agree that six weeks is way too early to start even simple foods like cereal. A baby's stomach and intestines aren't developed enough to handle solid foods before at least four to six months. At that age they can be introduced to rice cereal. The current thinking for breast-fed babies is not to wean them for a year.

That Was Then: As young parents, we were cautioned that responding too quickly and too often to our babies' cries would spoil them.

This Is Now: For the first few months of life, at least, a baby cannot be spoiled, experts claim. She's not crying with the intention of manipulating her parents; she's crying because she's trying to communicate. When her parents respond promptly and lovingly to her crying, they're building her trust and encouraging her development. She's learning that the people around her love and care for her.

Mini Milestones

Can you remember when your kids said their first words, or took their first steps, or cut their first teeth? We couldn't with our kids either (although we do remember the exact date when we saw the Beatles perform at old Comiskey Park in Chicago in 1965).

Fuzzy memories from your early parenting days make it difficult to know when to anticipate your grandchild's developmental milestones. To help you, here's a little primer on what to expect of a typical child during the first five years of life. This guide also includes ways that experts say you can enhance your grandchild's development.

Keep this in mind: Children are individuals with their own internal clocks that ring when they are ready to walk, talk, and dress themselves. It's unfair to compare the development of one child with another.

Throughout your grandchild's early development, you should interact with her as often as you can. That means hug, cuddle, and rock her; talk, sing, and read to her—and, above all, just love her and have fun!

The Infant

Your grandchild is learning to trust in someone who can be counted on for care, fun, protection, and limits. She's discovering her physical abilities and the new things around her. When her needs are met and she receives loving care in a stable environment, she gains trust in her new world.

Her sense of touch develops rapidly—and it's one she enjoys. According to a University of Miami study, the more babies are picked up, hugged, and massaged, the better they develop. Babies who are touched frequently sleep better and have faster-developing nervous systems than do other babies.

Her sense of smell is better than you think. When only a few days old, a breast-fed baby will turn toward a pad with her mother's scent or breast milk on it but not toward an unscented pad or a pad with milk from another woman.

Singing, cooing, and talking to your infant grandchild will encourage her to imitate the sounds she hears. Good hearing is the key to language development.

At 0–3 Months

Your grandchild likely will:

- lift her head
- follow a slowly moving object with her eyes
- laugh
- smile
- bring her hands together
- love to be touched
- see best when things are eight to twelve inches away (the distance of a nursing baby from her mother's face) because her sight is about 20/200

What you can do for your grandchild:

- Take every opportunity to massage her. Apply some pressure during the massage and use a small amount of baby oil to help your hands glide over her skin.
- Enjoy having her touch you back. Babies are comforted by laying their hands on others' hands and faces.
- Wear clothes with contrasting light-dark patterns. She prefers sights that have high contrast.
- Give support for her immature neck muscles when you're holding her.
- Buy stimulating toys for her to see and hear. Some good choices: a simple mobile for over the crib; an unbreakable,

smooth-edged mirror to attach to the side of the crib; a music box; and a prism to hang in the nursery window.

- Provide plenty of physical contact.
- Hold her close to your face.
- Talk to her in a high-pitched voice. She's attuned to that tone and is capable of distinguishing human speech from other sounds.
- Wear the same lotion or fragrance each time you visit to take advantage of her keen sense of smell. She might recognize your special scent.
- Provide floor time for her in order to exercise developing muscles.
- Avoid startling her when you greet her. Approach gently and respect her own space.

At 3–6 Months

Your grandchild likely will:

- hold her head in a stable position
- bear some weight on her legs when supported in a standing position
- sit without support
- roll from her back to her stomach
- look for a dropped object
- begin eating rice cereal and unseasoned, pureed fruits and vegetables (after four months)
- show that her ability to perceive detail has improved dramatically

What you can do for your grandchild:

- Buy her a well-designed crib gym that provides objects for her to swipe at, bat, or pull; teething rings; key chains; and clutch balls that are small enough to play with and too large to be swallowed.

- Observe her interacting with her world so you can get a fascinating glimpse inside that little mind of hers.
- Keep her on the routine that she and her parents have set when it comes to eating, sleeping, and playing times.
- Introduce her to nature by putting her in a backpack and taking her for a hike. (Make sure she has adequate back and head support.)

At 6–9 Months

Your grandchild likely will:

- make an effort to get an out-of-reach toy
- pull up to a standing position from a sitting position
- hold an object
- sit without support
- start cutting teeth
- play simple games
- start to drink from a trainer cup that has two handles and a snap-on lid
- recognize her name
- develop the ability to judge where a sound is coming from and turn her head to locate the sound
- roll from her stomach to her back
- crawl backward or forward
- begin babbling

What you can do for your grandchild:

- Allow her to feed herself (and be prepared for the mess).
- Play games with her such as peek-a-boo, this little piggy, and pattycake.
- Allow her to scoot around in her bare feet whenever or wherever it's safe and comfortable.

- Give her visual stimulation. Let her see her face in a mirror, show her fish swimming in an aquarium, and always make plenty of eye contact.

At 9–12 Months

Your grandchild likely will:

- walk while holding on to furniture
- stand momentarily on her own
- take her first steps
- say "mama," "dada," or other simple words at random
- start eating with a spoon
- point to body parts if asked
- climb up stairs
- learn to wave bye-bye
- enjoy undressing herself

What you can do for your grandchild:

- Baby-proof your house for a baby who can now stand and reach more things than she could before.
- Realize that she will be getting into things as she investigates her surroundings, so make sure the areas she is exploring are safe.
- Buy her bath toys, balls, books with stiff cardboard pages, and toys with uncomplicated dials, push-buttons, and levers.

At 12–18 Months

Your grandchild likely will:

- begin to walk well
- roll a ball
- begin to show some interest in toilet training
- display separation anxiety

- have her last set of toddler immunizations
- brush her teeth with a parent's help
- wear her first pair of shoes

What you can do for your grandchild:

- Offer her finger food when appropriate.
- Label objects verbally, such as, "That's your truck."
- Mention colors, such as, "Your shirt is red."
- Provide opportunities for her to have positive experiences away from her parents by taking her to do fun things.
- Introduce her to your favorite music, particularly music with a rhythmic, repetitive beat.

The Toddler

As a toddler, your grandchild is learning to do things on her own. She's exploring her environment and testing many new skills, such as talking and running. According to famed psychoanalyst Erik Erikson, this stage of life (ages two to four) is a quest for autonomy. The toddler begins to assert herself because she can walk and is talking more. She will tend to resist authority and seek her independence as an individual.

At 18–24 Months

Your grandchild likely will:

- walk up steps
- stack blocks at least four blocks high
- name at least six body parts
- wash and dry her hands
- understand the concept of "time-out"
- use a fork

What you can do for your grandchild:

- Provide outdoor play whenever possible.
- Offer opportunities for active play such as climbing, running, kicking a ball, and pulling a wagon.

At 24–36 Months

Your grandchild likely will:

- use more than fifty words
- combine words
- show an interest in playmates
- brush her teeth without help
- put on and take off her clothes by herself
- sleep in a child's bed rather than a crib
- ride a tricycle
- give up her pacifier
- be toilet trained

What you can do for your grandchild:

- Provide opportunities for one-to-one child play.
- Guide and encourage positive behaviors.
- Talk about colors, body parts, and names of familiar people.
- Praise her successes during toilet training.
- Avoid unnecessary power struggles and let her have small victories. That way, she'll have the satisfaction of feeling "I can do it."
- Provide experiences that help her explore the world around her.

The Preschooler

As a preschooler, your grandchild has formed trust and independence. Now she can move on to the more social and creative aspects of her development, which include friends and toys.

During this time, say experts, be patient and don't push her to hurry and grow up. Respect her own pace. And, oh yes, keep your sense of humor.

At Age 3

Your grandchild likely will:

- use Play-Doh or crayons without putting them in her mouth
- exhibit independence and sometimes refuse to go along with adult instructions
- throw a ball overhand
- speak in two or three sentences at a time
- dress with little help
- balance on one foot briefly
- copy a circle
- prepare a bowl of cereal
- identify at least four colors
- have all twenty early childhood teeth
- not want to take a daily nap

What you can do for your grandchild:

- Provide as many "real" choices as possible, such as, "Do you want to wear red socks or blue socks?"
- Encourage independence by letting her do more things for herself.
- Encourage examples of good behavior, such as picking up toys together.

- Provide small motor activities to foster prewriting skills such as molding Play-Doh, stringing beads, and tearing paper.
- Talk about letters, numbers, and colors with her.
- Teach her simple songs and nursery rhymes.
- Provide simple chores to build self-esteem, such as putting silverware away, folding washcloths, and dumping items in the trash.
- Talk to her about upcoming events and plans, such as, "Today we are going to the zoo."
- Encourage healthy habits, such as brushing teeth, washing hands, exercising, and eating nutritious foods.
- Make sure she gets plenty of sleep—twelve to fourteen hours per day when she's in your care.

At Age 4

Your grandchild likely will:

- prefer children to adults
- have imaginary friends
- be very active and enjoy running, jumping, and climbing
- refine her motor skills
- enjoy talking
- ask lots of questions
- have good bladder and bowel control

What you can do for your grandchild:

- Allow opportunities for her to play with other children.
- Treat her imaginary friends with respect.
- Provide crayons, markers, scissors, paint, etc.
- Be a good listener.
- Consider buying her a watch or calendar so you can mark special times and dates.
- Be understanding about occasional bladder/bowel accidents.

At Age 5

Your grandchild likely will:

- begin to care about others' opinions
- display reasoning ability
- have good control of her hands and legs
- display her preference for being right- or left-handed
- be affectionate and helpful
- enjoy making new friends
- want things to be "fair"
- pretend to write or read

What you can do for your grandchild:

- Talk about feelings: happy, sad, calm, surprised.
- Give explanations and reasons for rules.
- Encourage drawing and writing; say, "Tell me about your picture."
- Involve her in simple, supervised cooking activities.
- Be consistent with rules, routines, and expectations.
- Point out words in the environment that she may recognize, such as McDonald's, Discovery Zone, a stop sign, etc.
- Encourage her to interact with aunts, uncles, and cousins of all ages so she has a sense of belonging to more than her immediate family.

(The majority of the information on the various stages of development was adapted with permission from the Genesee County [Michigan] Strong Families/Safe Children's *Grandparent Guidebook.* We added additional material from other child development experts.)

Fifties and Sixties Songs to Sing to Your Grandchild for Fun

- "(We're Gonna) Rock Around the Clock"—Bill Haley and His Comets (1955)
- "Hound Dog"—Elvis Presley (1956)
- "The Purple People Eater"—Sheb Wooley (1958)
- "Witch Doctor"—David Seville (1958)
- "Alley Oop"—The Hollywood Argyles (1960)
- "Itsy Bitsy Teenie Weenie Yellow Polka Dot Bikini"— Brian Hyland (1960)
- "Do Wha Diddy Diddy"—Manfred Mann (1964)
- "The Name Game"—Shirley Ellis (1964)
- "Wooly Bully"—Sam the Sham and the Pharaohs (1965)
- "I'm Henry the Eighth (I Am)"—Herman's Hermits (1965)
- "Wild Thing"—The Troggs (1966)
- "The 59th Street Bridge Song (Feelin' Groovy)"— Harpers Bizarre (1967)
- "Born to Be Wild"—Steppenwolf (1968)
- "Yummy, Yummy, Yummy"—Ohio Express (1968)
- "Hair"—The Cowsills (1969)

Fifties and Sixties Songs to Sing to Your Grandchild at Night

- "All You Have to Do Is Dream"—The Everly Brothers (1958)
- "Catch a Falling Star"—Perry Como (1958)
- "The Lion Sleeps Tonight (Wimoweh)"—The Tokens (1962)
- "Blowin' in the Wind"—Peter, Paul and Mary (1963)

- "Puff the Magic Dragon"—Peter, Paul and Mary (1963)
- "Deep Purple"—Nino Tempo and April Stevens (1963)
- "Turn! Turn! Turn!"—The Byrds (1965)
- "Scarborough Fair/Canticle (Parsley, Sage, Rosemary and Thyme)"—Simon and Garfunkel (1966)
- "Cherish"—The Association (1966)
- "Mellow Yellow"—Donovan (1966)
- "There's a Kind of Hush"—Herman's Hermits (1967)
- "Dedicated to the One I Love"—The Mamas and the Papas (1967)
- "(Sittin' on) the Dock of the Bay"—Otis Redding (1968)
- "What a Wonderful World"—Louis Armstrong (1968)
- "El Condor Pasa (If I Could)"—Simon and Garfunkel (1970)

We Can Work It Out

Dealing with Your Adult Child

The toddler who displayed her Magic Marker talents by using the living room wall as a canvas, the grade schooler who ripped her Cabbage Patch Doll during a temper tantrum, the teenybopper who went hysterical over Duran Duran, the sophomore who failed to adequately explain the dent on your new car, has finally grown up to become a parent herself.

Seeing her tenderly cradle her infant, you can't help but wonder how this former tongue-pierced, back-talking, purple-haired alien will act as a loving, responsible mother. She's an adult now, which means she gets to call the shots concerning the care of her children. Still, it's difficult for you to stop parenting, just like it is for most of us.

We boomers have spent the last couple of decades telling our children to clean their rooms, brush their teeth, take driver's ed, get their degrees. Even though they're grown, it's only natural for us to keep right on telling them what to do. We speak from years of experience. Unfortunately, the new parents generally are not in the mood to listen.

We rationalize by claiming that all we want is the best possible care for our grandchildren, and, besides, the parents are so new at their job. But the reality is that they are grown up and in charge of their lives, family, and future. Whether we like it or not, they have their own way of doing things, which may go counter to our way of parenting. They get to choose their own style and make their own mistakes; they no longer are bound by our parenting beliefs and rules.

However, even though we know we must let go of the reins to our adult children, they are still our *children*. Forever. It doesn't matter how old any of us are.

> **Allan:** *"Here I am a grandfather, and my dad is still trying to tell me how to parent. For example, we were on a family outing last month on a brisk day, and he urged me to convince my daughter to put a jacket on my grandson. My dad got upset with me when I refused."*

The Don't Ask, Don't Tell Dilemma

Should you offer the new parents unsolicited advice if you honestly believe it's for the good of your grandchild, or should you do a Clarabelle and never say a word? Most experts believe you should clam up—but there is some wiggle room on this issue.

In most situations, suggests Dr. T. Berry Brazelton, you should bite your tongue. "When we see our children begin to act as parents, we get a little jealous—and competitive—and wish that they would do things our way," he explains. "But you can't tell your child, 'Do things my way.' That's very destructive to anybody's self-image. And competition like that undermines the grandchildren."

However, the noted pediatrician thinks that we boomers may have a tough time keeping our lips sealed. "Your generation was particularly narcissistic and you thought you knew everything." (You mean we *don't?*)

Margery Facklam in *Grandparents Today*: *"We wouldn't be rude enough to tell a friend how to feed her baby or how we feel about pacifiers. But we throw manners to the wind to impose our opinions on our children. We don't seem to think it strange to ask complex tax advice from an accountant-daughter and then tell her the next minute, 'You're starving this baby. When are you going to start giving him cereal?'"*

Dad on the Net: *"My parents give my wife and me a great deal of advice on how to discipline our kids, how to educate them, and even how to change diapers. But some of their advice is so outdated . . . they don't realize times have changed, kids have changed, and some of the old discipline techniques have changed for a reason. I want my parents to be involved, but right now they're too involved. But I don't want to put them off by saying anything for fear that they'll become less involved."*

"If you give your adult children unsolicited advice or suggestions, you have to be aware that you are undercutting them," says Dr. Brazelton. "They are liable to take it as criticism, no matter how well meant the advice is. It is wise for any grandparent to sit back and shut up and wait until the adult child turns to you. Otherwise, it can be destructive in most cases."

Such unsolicited advice often adds to the strain of an already stressed-out family, he says. Today's parents are overloaded with volumes of material on parenting. "The backlash of all the knowledge we have about child development and parenting is that parents today feel, 'Oh, gosh, everybody knows how to parent but me.' That puts them in a bind and [unwanted advice] only increases the stress, transmitting an even more stressful environment to the children."

Sue (Nana) Crawford: *"Chrisy will call me for advice, but when I give her advice, she doesn't want to hear it. Chrisy has read and read and read [parenting books] and I think she depends on them too much. With our generation, we went on instinct. We probably knew much less then than our [adult] children do now, but I think we did a decent job. I think young mothers almost have too much information."*

Ray (Papa) Villwock: *"When it comes to advice, they don't ask and I don't tell."*

"Grandparents can do much harm if they're not careful and aren't respectful of what their children are trying to do," says Dr. Brazelton. "Learning to parent is learning from mistakes, not from successes. Maybe the best thing a grandparent can do is watch the parents make mistakes then be ready to help them when they realize they've made a boo-boo.

"Remember that your job as a grandparent is to be supportive. If you really think that things need to be changed, sit down with your children and try to understand the reasons for the way they deal with their children."

Dad on the Net: *"I love my parents and want them to be a big part of our kids' lives. But I want them to respect our rules even when we're not there. My parents live nearby, so they see us often. They live on a lake, and we want the children [nonswimming toddlers] to wear PFDs [personal floatation devices] while out on the dock. My parents are offended if I mention this to them. . . . 'We wouldn't let anything happen to them!' Same fight about car seats. . . . 'We're careful drivers— never had an accident!' I think my mom thinks we just*

> sit around making up weird rules so that we are 'in
> control' of their relationships with the kids. Yes, we've
> tried explaining, to seemingly deaf ears, or at best, scorn
> for our position. And, after all, this is a control issue."

Sandi (Grammy) Kingman: *"I think my daughter is
super-cautious about safety concerning my two grandkids. However, I respect her wishes as a parent because
it eases her mind when she leaves the kids with me."*

Dr. Perry Buffington sees nothing wrong in offering advice—
if done in a loving, respectful manner. "It's difficult keeping your
mouth shut when your adult children do something you don't like,"
he says. "This is a common problem, especially among boomers
who are used to speaking up. However, there are ways to point out
concerns to your children without being argumentative. If you
say, 'Why in heaven's name are you doing that?' the 'why' word
will create such a defensiveness like hell hath no fury. The way I
would handle it is ask, 'Have you ever thought about doing it this
way or that way?' The grandparent takes on the role of teacher.
When you point out choices, you're in control, but the parents
think they are."

Dr. Buffington says you can show your concern without making
it look like interference by stating your case. "You say, 'I am concerned about this and here is why.' And then look for the remedy."
Don't push, he warns, because it will raise your child's hackles.
"Remember, the parent has the final say. If you as a grandparent
try to control everything, you are doomed to fail."

Adds Dr. Arthur Kornhaber, "You're a parent and a grandparent. Your children and their children look up to you as the head
and the heart of the family. As a grandparent, you have the responsibility to build the family and the family continuum, the family
ego, the family philosophy, the family values. That's important.

Don't meddle but certainly care and give advice. All through history, grandparents were the teachers and it doesn't stop now. You have lived longer than the kids. You know more."

> **Boomer G-Ma:** "*I voice my way of doing what I think is right. I guess even if they [her adult children] don't agree, it can't be that bad because they keep coming back for more. Aw, hell, they think I'm nuts and probably go along with me just to pacify me. Boy, have I got one over on them.*"

When dealing with the way Allison and Dan are raising our grandsons Chad and Danny, we pretty much repeat to ourselves the mantra "keep quiet." Sure, we'd do some things differently. But it doesn't matter. Chad and Danny are our grandsons, not our sons. We are not in charge of them, their parents, or their parenting. The moment we became grandparents, our relationship with Allison and Dan evolved to a different level.

Like every grandparent, we've had to learn diplomacy, tact, and a sensitivity to how our words and actions could affect our relationship with the parents. Whenever we get the urge to tell them what to do, which isn't very often, we simply think back to when we were new parents and how we felt when our parents tried to give us unsolicited advice. We hated it!

When Allison and Dan ask for our advice, we give our opinion and then leave it up to them (and suffer in silence when they decide our advice sucks).

> **Allan:** "*One of the biggest kicks I've had as a grandparent is watching Allison turn into a terrific mother. It's a real joy for me. She and Dan are doing such a great job that I seldom have the urge to offer suggestions on how to parent.*"

We tend to agree with Dr. Lillian Carson, who wrote in her book *The Essential Grandparent:* "Don't kid yourself by thinking that asking a question isn't really interference. I've done it myself only to realize later that I was not only expressing my concern but suggesting what I'd like them to do. Although it is more tactful to ask, 'Do you think you should call the doctor?' it is still a judgment. Even your tone of voice conveys a message. We must earn the right to voice our opinion by establishing a supportive relationship with praise, encouragement, and assistance."

> **Jane (Grandmom) Whitfield:** *"Do I ever see them [her adult children] make what I think is a mistake? Yes, but I keep my mouth shut. I know they are perfectly capable and they'll figure it out."*

> **Kathy:** *"As I was about to change Chad's diaper for the first time, I paused to admire my tiny newborn grandson. Mistaking my dawdling for hesitancy, my son-in-law, Dan, said, 'Let me show you how to do it.' I laughed inside. Here was this new father, who hadn't changed a diaper in his life until his son was born, telling me, a woman who has changed a million of them, how to do it. I let him show me. I enjoyed seeing the sense of accomplishment on his face after he put a diaper and sleeper on Chad and handed him to me. After Dan left the room, I turned Chad's jammies around. For some reason, fathers tend to put baby clothes on backward. I'll always remember the warm glow in Dan's eyes. I saw that same look in Allan's eyes the first time he changed Allison. And, yes, he put her clothes on backward too."*

Although most experts agree it's wise to express your opinions as infrequently as possible when it comes to the parenting of your grandchild, there are times when you absolutely need to voice your concern. If you are convinced that what the parent is doing has potential to harm the child emotionally or physically, you have an obligation to speak up.

"I believe that, while grandparents should not be intrusive, they should be forthcoming in identifying critical issues and be willing to help in difficult times," says Dr. Kornhaber. His Grandparent Study identified many grandparents who stepped in during troubled times to save children from drug-addicted or abusive parents.

The Family Hour

How well your advice is received often depends on how well you give it. "I believe in family conferences," says Dr. Kornhaber. "If I want to tell my son-in-law or daughter something, I'll take one of them out to lunch. I'm not going to say, 'You're a jerk for doing this.' I'm going to put it in a very loving, noncritical, and supportive way.

"People should sit down and lovingly let their feelings out and tell each other how they feel. I'll always give my opinion in a nice way—and I'm willing to accept my children's opinion. It's a two-way street. I don't think giving advice is meddling and controlling."

> **Tom (Grandpa) Andersen:** *"I read somewhere that when it comes to communicating between grandparents and their adult children, follow the example of your newborn grandchild: Let people know how you feel, rest, and spend lots of time listening."*

"Issues should be discussed," says Dr. Kornhaber. "Grandchildren have to understand that Mom and Dad and Grandma and Grandpa don't have to agree on everything, that conflict is normal, that problems are normal, that emotions are normal. You may have a fight, but if you're committed to each other, you come out the other end okay. It's great modeling for kids."

Here are some tips from experts on how to hold a family conference with your adult children:

- If you take the lead in opening the discussion, choose a time when nobody is tired or angry.
- Stick to one issue. Don't try to discuss a laundry list of problems.
- State your feelings or concerns as clearly as possible without attacking the parents.
- Find ways to compromise.
- Remain calm and treat each other with mutual respect.
- Don't belittle or undermine the confidence of the new parents. Instead, provide encouragement and sympathy.

"Allow everyone to express their feelings and point of view," says Dr. Kornhaber. "Indirect and roundabout communication gets nothing done. All it does is foment anger, frustration, and disappointment. Be direct and open with your feelings. Then come to an acceptable understanding. Usually everyone's love for the children involved can bring folks together."

When her daughter's doctor wanted to induce labor, nana-to-be Pat Connolly asked pointed questions that left the doctor irritated and her daughter confused. Here, with her permission, is what the cyber-columnist wrote about the experience:

An awkward situation was developing here and I definitely had something to say. But how do I say it? Or do I even say it? My son-in-law was very committed to the doctor's viewpoint. My daughter wasn't sure. And I thought more questions needed to be asked.

I recognized a dilemma that would come up again and again in life surrounding important decisions with my grown children. How much do I say? What was my motive? Was it to give them my viewpoint from years of experience or to make sure that they handled the situation my way? I could try to get them to do what I thought was right (as I had when they were children) or I could step back and let go of this phase of the parent-child relationship.

When we parents complained that our children didn't appear to grow up or make the right decisions, maybe there was something else going on that we failed to see. Maybe we continued to decide what they should or shouldn't do—and we let them know in subtle or not-so-subtle ways.

When I examined my point of view, I saw that this part of my job as a parent was done. Just as I would do for any friend, my job now was to tell my daughter and son-in-law what I thought, then step back and let them make their decision. It was time to let them know that I'll be there, but I won't interfere.

Not to impulsively act as a parent was very difficult. It was a new way of thinking for me. After all those years of raising them, I no longer had the final word. If I had continued in the old direction, there would be no growing in our relationship as adults. There might not even be a relationship, because most adults resent others interfering in their lives.

I sat down with my daughter and her husband and told them my thoughts and anxieties on inducing labor. Then I said, "I'll support whatever you decide." They decided to follow the doctor's advice. What could have been a disaster in our relationship was averted. I understand now that I can make life easier for my adult children and me if I can distinguish when I'm being the parent and when I'm being a friend.

Involvement versus Meddling

"A lot of grandparents pussyfoot around because they're afraid of meddling," says Dr. Kornhaber. "They try to be very sophisticated and not pushy, but they end up not making their wishes and needs known to the parents." As a result, he added, sometimes parents don't involve grandparents based on the mistaken assumption that the grandparents aren't interested in the family.

"Speak up," he suggests. "One of the problems is that there are too many elders and too many adult children who wrongly think grandparents' interest means meddling and advice means controlling. I hate that. Offering advice in a noncritical way and showing interest in the grandchildren means you're loving and supportive. Parents can always refuse the grandparents' advice.

"On the other hand, I hear parents say the grandparents don't care. The parents never offer to explain their needs. They don't want to ask Mom and Dad to baby-sit because they feel sorry for the grandparents. This kind of stuff stifles open communication."

> **Jane (Grandmom) Whitfield:** *"As the mother of married sons, I feel somewhat left out. While I communicate with the boys, men do not communicate to the extent women do. Men don't go into detail, and I love the details."*

> **Nana Pat:** *"I offer advice more to my son than to my daughter-in-law. I'll say to him, 'Now whatever you do, don't say anything to her,' because there's nothing worse than, 'My mom says this and this.'"*

As a grandparent, you never know how your comments will be received. When you think you are helping your children with sound suggestions, they may think you're meddling. If you don't offer advice, your children may think you don't care. So what do you do?

Suggests Dr. Buffington: "One of the best ways to avoid meddling when you want to help is to simply say, 'I want to do more but I'm afraid of meddling.' Honesty is always in order. Be adult. Don't play games. If you want to do or know something, ask. But be prepared for an answer that you don't want to hear.

"Usually, though, parents are often so overwhelmed they are looking for someone to help them. So if you happen to be standing there, make it known you're available. You'll get the chance to help out and improve your relationship with your adult child. Be there and show an interest in helping care for your grandchild."

> **Sue (Nana) Crawford:** *"I told [her daughter] Chrisy that I wouldn't baby-sit full-time. But I meet her and the kids [a toddler and an infant] and do things together. She and I also share a job working for my husband. I keep the kids when she works. It seems to help Chrisy to get out of the house."*

The parent-grandparent relationship often affects, and is affected by, the level of involvement in the family by the grandparent.

"When grandparents are involved with grandchildren, it really helps marriages," says Dr. Kornhaber. "It takes a lot of the pressure off because the parents may be able to go off alone for a weekend or a vacation. It shows that the grandparents are still loving parents."

> **Mom on the Net:** *"My husband's parents live only twenty minutes away. It seems that we only see them for special occasions, and although we have invited them over and occasionally asked for baby-sitting help, they never seem to have the time. Okay, but I don't want to hear any whining that 'my grandchildren don't know me.'"*

"According to many parents in our Grandparent Study, not only were they missing their parents' involvement, but the grand-children were too," Dr. Kornhaber reports. "One young mother sadly complained that her own father lived two blocks away yet never took the time to spend more than an occasional hour with her children. When I spoke with this grandfather he said that he didn't want to 'meddle' in his daughter's life. He thought that he was doing his daughter a favor by allowing her to be 'independent.'

"One of the most frequent reasons for grandparent-parent non-involvement is lack of communication. Many parents are hesitant about asking their parents to be more involved because they feel guilty about doing so. A young father told me, 'My parents have worked hard all of their lives. I don't have the right to ask them to get involved in mine.' The truth is, however, that young parents do have a right to at least ask their own parents for time and attention. Parents are parents for the rest of their lives.

"Some grandparents don't want to become involved even if they are asked. As one uninvolved grandmother said, 'I raised my kids and now I want time for myself.' Her son thought she was very selfish and self-centered. Under these circumstances the only thing an 'abandoned' parent can do is to involve a third party— a friend, a clergyperson, a therapist—to sit down with the family."

Playing by the Rules

Barbara Bowman, president of the Erikson Institute, believes it's counterproductive to keep silent if the rules for the grand-children in your house are different than those at your adult child's. "If you're sweating under the collar and it just makes you furious, then it's crazy to keep your mouth shut," she says. "You need to sit down and communicate in an honest, tactful way. Families work best when people have mutual respect and can find solutions together.

"My daughter and I agreed that when my granddaughter is at my house, she obeys my rules. For instance, at her home she can put her feet on the table. When she's at my house, her feet go under the table. She quickly learned what she can do at home and at her grandmother's. There are things she can do at my house that she can't do at home. I give her much more freedom when playing by herself. But I'm more a stickler for manners."

> **Alisa (Nana) Dollar:** *"I don't agree with [the discipline method] 'time-out,' but I adhere to the method when I keep the grandchildren. I have them for such a short time, so I follow the rules."*

> **Papa on the Net:** *"The parents let them [his grandchildren, ages two and four] run wild at home, but I don't in my house. I have no problem setting rules when they come over. They might as well learn now that their behavior at home isn't necessarily going to be tolerated elsewhere, like when they start school."*

Dr. Brazelton suggests that you exercise some restraint when disciplining the grandkids. "You don't want to endanger what your own children are doing with their children. Don't get into it, but if you must, you'd better have thought out how you want to handle discipline. If you're impulsive and overreact, you'll lose respect and might do something you don't believe in."

To build trust with your adult child, you need to play by his or her rules—most of the time, says Dr. Buffington. "If the parent says, 'I don't let my child have cookies,' don't give him cookies. However, every once in a while you should violate the rule just a little bit and whisper, 'Don't tell your mother.' It's like a secret bonding that every child remembers with his grandparents. You want that to happen occasionally. The truth is the parent wants you to do that too."

Doing It Again—Only Better

Occasionally we nanas and papas might lash out at a behavior that we helped cause, says Dr. Buffington. "Sometimes the parents don't know any other way to behave. When you see the adult child behave this way, you think, 'Oh, God, that's the way I taught him.' You see yourself—and that can be very painful.

"Sometimes when I counsel young parents, they say, 'I don't want suggestions from my parents or in-laws on parenting.' I reply, 'Get a grip. Your wish will never happen.' You never miss the water till the well runs dry. What the parents are really saying is 'I don't want the grandparents controlling my kid.' That's what they're most afraid of."

Because of painful memories of their own childhood, some parents are reluctant to let the grandparents too close to the grandkids, says Dr. Kornhaber. "During counseling sessions, I've had parents say, 'Well, my parents screwed me up during my childhood, so they'll screw up my kids.' I reply, with some seriousness, 'No they won't because now they know they screwed you up and they aren't going to let that happen again.'"

According to the Grandparent Study, in their relationships with their grandchildren, 68 percent of the grandparents reported they tended not to repeat the same mistakes they had made with their own children. "It was as if they learned from their experience and nature gave them another chance," says Dr. Kornhaber. Even their adult children felt the grandparents had displayed much better parenting skills now than when they were parents.

Many young dads are surprised to see their once-domineering, punitive fathers become old softies around their grandchildren. Erik Erikson wrote that grandparenting was an opportunity for men to make peace with their child-rearing pasts. In an Australian study, grandfathers reported enjoying their grandchildren more than their own sons and saw their involvement as a way to make up for lost opportunities with their own children. The benefits may span generations: By watching their once-distant fathers with their grandchildren, men may vicariously enjoy what they themselves missed years before—and relieve some of their lingering resentment.

You might actually get gently chided by the parents for being such a doting grandparent. "If your adult daughter or son says, 'You were never that nice to me,' don't resent it," says Dr. Brazelton. "They are recognizing that you have learned something since they were kids. Graciously acknowledge you have learned a thing or two in your time."

Staying Tight with the Gatekeepers

Your relationship with your adult child can have a profound affect—good or bad—on your grandchild.

"It's real simple," says Dr. Buffington. "Because the parents technically control access to the grandchild and are the gatekeepers, it's important for you to develop a good relationship with the gatekeepers."

If you're on excellent terms with your adult child, it's likely you'll have a good relationship with your grandchild. However, says Dr. Kornhaber, "even if you have a bad relationship with your adult child, you can still have a good one with your grandchild— if you spend time alone with him. But if Mom is there and you aren't getting along with her, the poor kid gets the fallout."

The experts agree that you should never talk to your grandchild in a negative way about his parents. It won't help him and could only make matters worse for you.

"The adults all have to love the kid more than they bug each other," says Dr. Kornhaber. "The parents are the linchpin of the relationship and really control a lot of it. But if you just leave the grandparent and the grandchild alone, for the most part it's wonderful. If the parents don't get along with the grandparents, the parents have to understand that it has nothing to do with the relationship between the grandparent and the grandchild.

"Every family should find ways for the grandparent to spend time alone with the grandchild because that relationship is a separate human connection. The best thing parents can do is to get out of the way and tell the kid to go off with Grandma and Grandpa and have a good time."

Walk Right In

When Your Grandchild Visits

When our grandsons Chad and Danny come to visit, we put our life on hold and go into what we call our Grandkid Mode. We spring into action and prepare ourselves and our house for their arrival—or, more aptly, their invasion.

First, we reschedule or cancel any social plans and other appointments, and we inform our friends we'll be out of the loop during our grandsons' stay. Most everything comes to a halt—including a few days of work, because we try to create as much free time as possible for them. Total focus goes to Chad and Danny.

Mentally, we know what will happen to our house. It will be trashed: toys scattered everywhere—under the dining room table, behind the curtains, between the couch cushions. Sticky fingerprints on walls, windows, and appliances. Spit-up, drool, and Juicy Juice on chairs, floors, and carpets. We accept the fact that the moment they enter into our house, all sense of order walks out. No matter what plans we make, we are prepared to call an audible and change them in case one of them takes too long a nap, or is too sick, or is in one of those moods. But we love their visits for no other reason than we get to be with our grandsons.

We pull out the boxes marked "Grandkids." One box contains picture books; another has art supplies, including butcher paper, crayons, markers, watercolors, and paste; one is full of videos; and another has simple games, puzzles, and cards. Then we bring out the toy box. Instead of one made of brightly colored molded plastic, ours is a maple blanket bench that fits in with our decor. Although it was designed to keep blankets in, we use it to store toys that we've collected from friends and relatives. The lid has a child-safety hinge so it won't fall down when opened.

We're from the "hide everything" school. We sweep through the house like frenzied burglars and gather all the breakable or unsafe items that we don't want the boys to touch. We put these things out of their reach and sight. That way we don't have to fret over the fate of breakable objects and we don't have to say "no" to the boys so many times.

Some grandparents leave their possessions out and try to teach their grandkids how to respect the items. But that takes alertness, composure, and effort on your part, and it only works if your grandchild frequently visits. But be prepared for the inevitable accidents. If there's an object that's priceless to you, put it away during the visit.

> **Sue (Nana) Crawford:** *"When the grandchildren come, we stay in the family room, which can be closed off from the rest of the house. It's child-proofed and we have all the toys in there. My living room and dining room are full of crystal and other fragile things. Having one room a mess is easier to clean up and to get back to normal."*

Dr. Arthur Kornhaber believes that the grandparents' house should be a second home for the grandkids—a getaway to explore, rummage through family memorabilia, encounter the unexpected, and celebrate holidays with the whole family. "The grandparents' home can serve as the center of the family and can keep family members in communication with each other," he says.

"Create a special place for your grandchildren in your home—a place that is theirs alone and where they can do no wrong. For toddlers, childproof your home appropriately. Remove all breakables and dangerous materials. Store the good china. Create a space where youngsters can roam freely without getting into mischief.

"Provide a shelf for children's books, a special place to sleep, a place to horse around. Find out their favorite games, and buy them. Then practice so you can play with them.

"Reserve a special place in the food pantry and the refrigerator for food and snacks and label a container with each child's name. Have things they like."

Get an old dresser and designate a drawer for each grandkid. Inside put fun items such as old clothes, hats and purses, junk jewelry, puzzles, a magnifying glass, magnets, and dozens of inexpensive things that you can find at a drugstore or flea market. Let the grandkids know they each have their very own drawer. When they visit, they'll eagerly open it to see what's new inside. Your challenge will be to change the contents as the kids get older.

Child-Proofing Your Home

When our first grandchild, Chad, was three months old, he came to our house for his first visit. We had forgotten how much preparation is needed to provide a healthy, safe environment for an infant.

After reading the safety guidelines from the Consumer Product Safety Commission (CPSC), we discovered that our house was a virtual danger zone for him. Adding to our concern were these sobering stats from the CPSC: More children die in home accidents than from all childhood diseases combined. And more than one-third of all potentially harmful or fatal childhood poisonings occur in the homes of children's *grandparents*.

To safeguard your home for the little one, you must be as diligent and vigilant as Sergeant Joe Friday. Too often, when young children visit, we tend to worry about what the kids might do to our things rather than what the things might do to the kids. Just ask yourself, what's more precious to you—your Limoges collection or your grandchildren? Evaluate the environment of your home in light of their safety.

"You're constantly sweating it when you have very young children around," admits Barbara Bowman, president of the Erikson Institute. "You must be more vigilant than ever. I found I'm much more careful with my granddaughter than I ever was with my own child. I would die if anything would happen to her on my watch."

If you want to gain more confidence in yourself as a baby-sitter, take a Red Cross course on infant and child CPR and standard first aid.

Before our grandsons arrive at our house, we get down on all fours and take a toddler's-eye view of each room to check for any dangers. We usually find something that poses a possible risk. Before their last visit, we discovered a cat toy lodged under the couch but within a child's reach and a ballpoint pen inadvertently left as a bookmark in a magazine on the coffee table.

> **Congressman Dave Hobson:** *"After having raised three children, my wife Carolyn and I are both dusting off our baby-wrangling skills and we are starting by making our home safe for little ones."*

If your grandchild is a toddler or an active crawler, heed the following guidelines suggested by the CPSC and other safety-conscious organizations. Most of these tips involve common sense, but they are helpful reminders. (Hey, airline pilots go through a checklist before every flight, so why shouldn't nanas and papas go through one before every grandchild visit?)

Around the house:

- Place sturdy safety gates at the top and bottom of the stairs. Gates with small diamond-shaped openings are best since they can't entrap small fingers like accordion-style gates.
- Keep all insect spray, weed killers, gasoline, paint products, bleaches, soaps, detergents, oven and drain cleaners, polishes, fabric softeners, bluing agents, and stain treatment sprays in their original containers and in a secure cabinet.
- Keep all thin plastic wrapping materials, such as dry cleaning, produce, or trash bags out of your grandchild's reach. Never use thin plastic material to cover mattresses or pillows because the plastic film can cling to her face, causing suffocation.
- Guard against electrical shocks by covering unused outlets with safety caps.

Michelle (Grammy) Davies: *"Nothing is toddler-proof. Before my two-year-old grandson came over to my new house, I covered the electrical outlets. He wasn't there thirty minutes when he brought me a handful of outlet covers."*

- Keep your grandchild away from open windows and screens to prevent a fall. Screens are designed to keep insects out, not kids in. Avoid placing furniture near windows so she can't climb out the window.
- Lock lower windows and block them so they can't be opened more than six inches.
- Always use restraining straps with an infant carrier seat. Don't place the carrier seat on any soft, unstable surfaces.

- If you have a swimming pool, install a fence or barrier surrounding all four sides with self-closing and self-latching gates. If the house is part of the barrier, all doors leading from the house to the pool should be protected with an alarm and locks.
- Use safety latches for kitchen, bathroom, and workshop cabinets.
- Make sure your floors are smooth and have nonskid surfaces. Rugs should be skid-proof.

Glen Ecklund: *"Watch out for wastebaskets! Ours is locked away under the sink, but Ethan still managed to transfer a couple of spoons from the dishwasher to it. We were lucky to notice them while taking out the trash. However, Madeleine's keys are long gone."*

- Make sure pipes, radiators, fireplaces, wood-burning stoves, and other hot surfaces can't be reached by your grandchild.
- Cushion fireplace edges with commercial corner guards.
- Never drink coffee, tea, or any other hot liquid when holding your grandchild.
- Never tie pacifiers or other items around the baby's neck. Cords and ribbons can become tightly twisted, or can catch on crib corner posts or other protrusions, causing strangulation.
- Keep your grandchild away from common toxic house plants such as daffodils, delphinium, dieffenbachia, hydrangeas, philodendrons, poinsettias, lilies of the valley, caladium, and foxglove. For a complete list contact your local poison control center.
- Make sure all interior doors can be easily unlocked and opened from the outside in case your grandchild locks herself inside a room.

Kathy: *"When Chad was fifteen months old, he managed to lock himself in the bathroom at home. Allison was worried that he would somehow fall in the toilet or hurt himself in some way. After fifteen tense minutes, his dad finally sprang the old lock with a screwdriver. They found Chad covered from head to toe in toilet paper."*

- If you let your grandchild play outside, first check the area and clean up any debris, sharp objects, or pet droppings.
- Have handy the phone number of your local poison control center, a pediatrician, and other emergency numbers.
- Have first-aid materials and simple medications on hand, such as Band-Aids, antibacterial salve, thermometer, antidiarrhea preparations, and ice packs.
- Obtain an emergency medical-release form giving you the authority to approve medical care for your grandchild if the parents are away. (For more details, see chapter 9.)

Diane Willis: *"People should be really careful of the rubber tips on doorstops. I couldn't believe Nick crawled all around the house and stripped them off every single doorstop. We then removed the doorstops from the wall because the sharp points where the rubber tip goes could injure Nick."*

In the bathroom:

- Store electrical equipment such as curling irons, hair dryers, and razors away from water and from your grandchild's reach. Make sure they're disconnected when not in use.

- Keep cleaning products, disinfectants, cosmetics, powders, fingernail preparations, hair-care products, mouthwash, and medicine locked in a cabinet or out of your grandchild's reach.
- Don't throw shaving products like disposable razors and other potentially dangerous objects into the wastebasket. Wrap them in toilet paper and put them directly into the garbage.
- Keep all perfumes, cosmetics, powders, and sachets out of your grandchild's reach.
- Set the water heater temperature at between 110 and 120 degrees Fahrenheit to help prevent scalding. Always check bathwater temperature with your wrist or elbow before putting your grandchild in to bathe. If you want to be supersafe, buy an antiscalding device, which ranges in price from $15 to $75, not including installation.
- At bath time, fill the tub with just enough water to cover your grandchild's legs.
- Never leave your grandchild alone or with a youngster in the bath even for a few seconds. If the phone rings, don't answer it. It can't be as important as the safety of your grandchild.
- And for all you grandfathers, here's the hardest safety tip of all: Keep the toilet seat—and cover—down. (And, for extra safety, install a toilet seat latch.)

In the nursery:

- Put your grandchild to sleep on her back or side in a crib with a firm, flat mattress and no soft bedding underneath her. Studies indicate this will reduce the risk of suffocation and Sudden Infant Death Syndrome (SIDS). And if you're thinking of putting the baby in bed with you and your spouse, forget it. Infants have suffocated under sleeping adults who've rolled over.

- Never let the infant sleep on an adult bed because she can become trapped between the bed and the wall and suffocate.
- Never place the baby's crib or furniture near cords for window blinds or curtains. An infant can strangle on the loop of the cord.
- Keep cords out of reach by tying them to themselves or by using clamps, clothespins, cleats, or tie-down devices. Also, consider tying or hanging cords at or near the top of the window coverings.
- To prevent choking, take rattles, squeeze toys, teethers, and other toys out of the crib when the baby sleeps.
- Remove all crib toys that are strung across the crib when your grandchild is beginning to push up on her hands and knees or is five months old, whichever occurs first.

In the kitchen:

- When the baby is in a highchair, always use all safety straps to prevent her from climbing out, falling, or sliding under the tray. Don't leave her alone for even a minute.
- Use your stove's back burners and turn the pot handles inward whenever possible.
- Keep your grandchild away from tablecloths, so she can't pull down hot foods or liquids on herself.

Gran Nan: *"We learned the hard way not to have tablecloths around when our granddaughter Bree visits. When she was sixteen months old, she yanked on a tablecloth to pull herself up and knocked over a vase that conked her on the head."*

- Keep all countertop appliances, such as the toaster or coffeemaker, away from the edge. Keep them unplugged when not in use.
- Lock up household cleaning products, knives, matches, and plastic bags, or keep them on shelves in upper cabinets.

Gramma Kay: *"Look in your kitchen drawers. Besides the obvious like knives, you should put boxes of foil and plastic wrap out of reach. Our grandson Trevor cut his hand on the sharp edge of one of those boxes. I felt so sick to my stomach because his safety was my responsibility and I let him down. It was hard for me to face his parents."*

Bob (Boppy) Giavonni: *"Beware of oven doors. When our granddaughter Gillian was about two, she walked by the hot oven and yanked open the door. I hadn't run across the room that fast since I grabbed the last beer at a frat party."*

Toys and toy chest:

- Check that all playthings you give your grandchild are safe—especially hand-me-downs and garage-sale specials.
- Throw away any toys that have lead-based paint, removable parts less than one-and-one-quarter inches long, or have sharp edges, corners, or protrusions.
- Keep small objects out of your grandchild's reach. Uninflated balloons, tiny toys, and toys with small, removable parts can be swallowed or become lodged in her windpipe, ears, or nose. Check to see that toys have not broken or come apart at the seams, exposing small

pellets that might be swallowed or inhaled. Even such common items as coins, pins, buttons, and small batteries can choke a child. If you're wondering if a toy or object is small enough, try dropping it into a tube from an empty roll of toilet paper. If it falls through, then the object is potentially dangerous.

- When choosing toys, look for labels that give age recommendations such as "Recommended for Children Three to Five Years Old." Some toys or games that are safe for older children may contain small parts that are hazardous in a younger child's hands.

- If a toy chest, trunk, or other container for storing toys has a free-falling lid, remove the lid. Otherwise it can drop accidentally on your grandchild's head or neck. Look for a chest that has supports to hold the lid open at any position, or choose one with sliding panels or a lightweight, removable lid.

- Get a spring-loaded lid-support device that will keep a lid from falling on your grandchild or from closing and trapping her inside. This device costs about $7.50 and should be used on all chests and trunks. Also, make sure the toy chest has air holes in the side in case she falls in.

Ken Meinken: *"I used to be a volunteer EMT. One of my early life squad runs was on a young child [put to bed for a nap] who got out of bed and crawled into the toy box and fell asleep there. He never awoke. Despite our CPR efforts and the hospital's efforts, he couldn't be revived. Although it's been fifteen years and a thousand other emergency runs have come and gone, I still shudder every time I see an unventilated toy box in a store."*

Handling Food

When feeding your grandchild, first test all warmed foods for a comfortable eating temperature before serving. Heating baby food in a microwave is convenient, but many experts advise against it because it often leaves hot spots in the food that can burn your grandchild's mouth. If you do use a microwave, make sure you stir the food from the center out after heating to ensure that the temperature is even. Bottles of milk should never be microwaved because of hot spots. It's best to run the bottles under warm tap water (but never in boiling water).

When your grandchild begins eating solid foods at between four and eight months old, don't give her small, hard foods. They could lodge in her throat and cause her to suffocate. Wait until she's older or ask her parent when it's safe for her to eat nuts, chunky peanut butter, whole grapes, fruits with seeds or pits, breads with large pieces of grain, hard candy, popcorn, small slices of raw vegetables, and whole hot dogs.

Newborns and children under one year old are more vulnerable to food poisoning because of undeveloped immune systems. Even a small dose of harmful bacteria can make a tiny baby sick. Don't give her leftover formula or milk from a previous feeding, because harmful bacteria from the baby's mouth can get into the formula, where it can grow and multiply even after refrigeration and reheating.

If using commercial baby foods, check to see that the safety button on the lid is down. If the jar lid doesn't "pop" when opened, don't use it. Discard jars with chipped glass or rusty lids. Also remember not to feed the baby straight from a jar of baby food. Saliva on the spoon can contaminate the remaining food. Transfer food from the jar to a bowl before feeding the baby.

Honey is a no-no for babies because of the potential of infant botulism. Honey should not be given to, or used in foods for, infants under the age of one. Below this age, infants don't have adequate stomach acid to inactivate botulinal spores.

Remember how you let your kids eat raw cookie dough or raw cake batter? Experts now say that's risky because the raw eggs in the mixture can lead to food-borne illness from salmonella poisoning.

Careful hand washing, especially with antibacterial soap, is one of the best ways to stop germs from spreading. As soon as your grandchild can understand, stress hand washing after going to the bathroom and before eating.

Baby bottles, nipples, screw caps, and covers all should be carefully washed, air dried, and stored until needed. Filled bottles and open cans of formula should be kept in the refrigerator. Filled bottles should be used within twenty-four hours, open cans within forty-eight hours. To prevent bacterial growth, don't leave the baby's bottle out of the refrigerator for longer than two hours and throw away any formula left after a feeding.

Pets

Your dog, cat, or pet gecko might not be accustomed to the noise and actions of your grandchild. Honestly assess your pet's personality to see how well it can tolerate the intrusion of a young child. If the animal can't handle the situation, put it outside, in the basement, or in a room during the visit. Otherwise, use care and patience when introducing your pet to her. If your grandchild is old enough, teach her how to approach the animal. Never leave her alone with any dog, cat, or other pet.

Also, be sure you store the pet food out of your grandchild's reach. And don't leave any out in a bowl on the floor. Some kinds of dry food are perfect choking size for a crawling baby.

Baby Equipment

If your infant grandchild visits you, you need at the very least a crib or Pack 'N Play, a high chair, a car seat, and a stroller.

It's often impractical for the parents to lug all that baby equipment, especially when flying, so you have several choices: You can buy used items at swap meets or garage sales; purchase new equipment; borrow stuff from friends or neighbors; or drag out the things you last stored in the attic during the Ford administration.

That last choice can be a problem because much of the equipment we used when our kids were little is considered too dangerous today. In fact, after hearing tips from experts and seeing the latest products for infants, you wonder how our kids survived babyhood. Virtually everything we used back then—the windup swing with chain-link supports, the wobbly walkers, the wide-slatted cribs—is not only obsolete but a potential child-maimer or killer.

When choosing used or new baby equipment, check for poor construction, instability, missing parts, and excessive wear. Most manufacturers have a toll-free number and will offer replacement parts and instructions. Avoid getting equipment that has any exposed screws, bolts, or fasteners with sharp edges or points; also avoid scissor-like mechanisms that could crush fingers.

If you're wondering if a new or used product is safe, look for a tag or sticker that says it is certified by the Juvenile Products Manufacturers Association (JPMA) or the American Society for Testing and Materials (ASTM). Stringent standards have been developed for high chairs, play yards (what we used to call play pens), walkers, strollers, gates and enclosures, full-size cribs, and portable hook-on chairs.

Crib

Have you been saving your children's old crib for your grand-children? Unless it meets national safety standards, keep it in the attic as an heirloom or use it for kindling.

Each year, according to the CPSC, about fifty babies suffocate or strangle when they become trapped between broken crib parts or in cribs with older, unsafe designs.

> **Congressman Dave Hobson:** *"I learned that the crib my three children used is actually considered unsafe for infants and we are buying a new one in time for our next visit from grandchildren."*

According to the CPSC, a safe crib has:

- no missing, loose, broken, or improperly installed screws, brackets, or other hardware on the crib or the mattress support
- no missing slats
- no more than $2^3/_8$ inches between crib slats, so the baby's body can't fit through the slats (Here's an easy way to measure: Try passing an upright soda can be-tween the slats. If the can goes through, the slats are spaced too far apart, so get rid of the crib.)
- a firm, snug-fitting mattress so the baby can't get trapped between the mattress and the side of the crib (You should not be able to get more than two adult fin-gers in the space between the mattress and the sides of the crib.)
- no corner posts over $1/_{16}$ of an inch above the end panels (unless they are over sixteen inches high for a canopy), which could snag the baby's clothes and strangle her

- no cutout areas on the headboard or footboard that could trap the baby's head
- a mattress support that doesn't easily pull apart from the corner posts so the baby can't get trapped between the mattress and crib; mattress support hangers should be secured by closed hooks
- no cracked or peeling paint
- no splinters or rough edges

Safety seat

During your grandchild's visit, you'll need a child safety seat. Many hospitals rent seats, and several auto insurance companies subsidize new purchases. If you're planning on buying a new car, consider getting one with built-in child seats. Although more expensive, convertible seats—which face toward the rear for infants and forward for toddlers—can be a better buy in the long run.

Most states have a child passenger protection law requiring small children (usually up to age four or forty pounds) to ride in approved child safety seats. The best way to transport your grandchild is in a child safety seat in the rear middle seat of your car.

From birth until your grandchild weighs twenty pounds, use an infant or convertible seat facing the rear of the vehicle to provide the most protection. Don't place a car seat in the front seat of a vehicle that has an air bag on the passenger side.

Use only a child safety seat that meets Department of Transportation (DOT) requirements. The seat should have a stamp showing it was manufactured after January 1, 1981, and carry a label that says, "This child restraint system conforms to all applicable federal motor vehicle safety standards."

Other baby equipment

Here are more tips from the CPSC:

- Make sure the portable, umbrella-type stroller pushes smoothly and easily and has a three-point safety strap. If you live in a sunny climate, use a canopy.
- Look for high chairs that have two safety straps—a waist strap and a crotch strap. Never depend upon the feeding tray to restrain or protect your grandchild. Instead, secure the straps.
- Don't use a play yard with holes in the netting larger than 1/4 inch or with wooden slats further than 2 3/8 inches apart. (Try the soda can test.) With a wood play yard, check for any missing or loose staples. And make sure it's properly opened and locked.
- Don't use a mesh-sided portable crib with a side left down. Such a position can pose a serious hazard because the mesh forms a loose pocket into which your infant grandchild can roll and suffocate. Also, don't add a pillow or a mattress that is deeper than one inch.
- If your grandchild is in a baby walker, keep her away from areas where there are uneven floors such as carpet edges or raised thresholds that may cause the walker to tip over.

If you don't already have one, get a portable phone and keep it with you when you're watching or bathing your grandchild. That way, if you get a phone call, she never has to leave your sight. Let's face it, no matter what precautions you take to child-proof your home, absolutely nothing is safer for your grandchild than you keeping your eye on her at all times.

I've Got to Get a Message to You

The Long-Distance Grandparent

If you're a long-distance grandparent, you can still enjoy a meaningful relationship with your grandkid and play an important role in his life. It doesn't matter if you live on Alaska's North Slope and he hails from the Florida Keys. You can be close to him.

The secret is to promote yourself with a Cassius Clay vigor. Long before he became Muhammad Ali, he made his impact on the world by brashly hyping himself. (Okay, so he had a wicked right too.) He refused to let the world ignore him.

Don't let your faraway grandchild ignore you—and don't you ignore him. Despite the distance, you can make an impact in his life in dozens of different ways, showing him how much he means to you. With today's technology, it's easier than ever for you to stay in touch with your grandkid and display your love, concern, values, sense of humor, and family history.

"There is absolutely no excuse for out of sight, out of mind," declares sociologist and family expert Susan Newman. "You have e-mail, faxes, video phones, and telephone."

It might take more effort, imagination, and creativity to grandparent from a different state, but you can be nearly as effective as the grandparent who lives down the street. The key is to keep in touch on a regular basis with your grandkid as you learn about him and he learns about you. Making your presence (in spirit) known strengthens your ties with him and reminds him that he is in your thoughts every day.

> **Jackie Quiram:** *"Being a long-distance grandmother means taking every opportunity to make a connection. Over the years, what you share together with grandchildren adds up to lots of rich experiences."*

It's a whole lot easier to pull off if you have a decent relationship with the parents. If they don't help, your efforts to stay close to your grandchild are much harder. From the start, your adult children need to know how important it is for you to stay in touch with him. The parents need to talk about you (hopefully in a positive light) to him. They need to constantly reinforce in the child how much you care about him. Nag the parents to help your promotion campaign. Use guilt, bribery, threats, whatever. Hey, this is your grandchild connection. It can't work very well without the parents' cooperation.

Through phone, letters, videos, e-mail, and other means, you can share your world with your grandchild. It sets the stage for those wonderful times when you're finally face to face with him. You won't have to get reacquainted because you aren't meeting as strangers; you're just enhancing an already blossoming relationship.

"Make your presence known in ways so simple that they'll become automatic," says Newman. "Small gestures frequently are the most meaningful."

E-Mail

Get on-line with your distant grandchild.

If you both have computers and access to e-mail, you can enjoy almost instantaneous communication. You can exchange daily messages, riddles, and jokes and play a variety of on-line games with your grandchild, depending on his age.

The computer offers grandparents unprecedented opportunities to live a fuller and more influential life with their grandchildren, says Dr. Arthur Kornhaber. "Your ability to be computer literate will exponentially augment your grandparent power.

"With e-mail you can keep in close touch with family members and, because of the ability to communicate in an ongoing manner, become a part of their everyday lives—no matter how far you live from one another. This idea of being able to knit family ties over distances is one of the happiest—and unexpected— findings of our own research in this field. Your computer can help you become the heart of your family more than ever before. Your options for creativity will be infinite."

> **Stan (Papa) Twilliger:** *"I picked up a children's joke book at the store and most every day when I'm in the office, I e-mail my grandson Michael a joke. His mom works at home so she finds the joke on her e-mail and reads it to him. He knows it's from Papa. His mom often e-mails me back with a comment or some funny thing that Michael said or did in preschool or at home."*

> **Harry (Papa) Yeatts:** *"Though our granddaughter is too young to read e-mail, her mom uses it to let us know the little things our granddaughter is up to. And we ask our daughter to pass on our love and to ask her questions. This way we get to keep up with daily happenings. Also, our daughter and son-in-law record our granddaughter's storytelling and singing on their computer and e-mail it to us. It makes a fine startup/exit sound file."*

Use the Internet to download and/or forward pictures, cute messages, and cartoons to your grandchild. Try sending electronic personalized greeting cards to him. In most cases, it doesn't cost anything to e-mail a personalized e-card. The Internet is chock full of services offering free e-cards. To find these services, go to your search engine and type in "electronic greeting cards" or "e-cards."

You can design and customize your own e-cards using various multimedia shareware and freeware programs that let you use your own message and voice. Many such programs contain graphics with built-in animation, synthesized speech, music, sound, and text/graphic buttons. You can download shareware and freeware through the Internet or through the software library of your own on-line service such as AOL or CompuServe.

You might consider creating your own personal Web page where you or your grandchild's parents can keep your far-flung relatives up to date on what's going on in everyone's lives. It's another way to help your grandchild grasp the concept of being connected with family members from all over the country (or world, for that matter). Many on-line services offer their subscribers a way to build their own free home page. If you want to make a more creative Web site, you can buy special software or sign up with a network of personal home pages that will build and store your personal Web site on its domain for a relatively modest annual fee.

Digital Cameras

The new-model digital cameras allow you to see excellent color pictures of your long-distance grandchild on your computer within minutes after they were shot. Although pricey (from about $500 to over $1,000), they are as easy to use as conventional point-and-shoot film cameras.

Digital cameras have a built-in liquid-crystal display that lets you immediately see what you've just shot. And unlike film cameras, if you don't like the results, you can delete them. The picture-editing software that comes with these cameras lets you easily correct for such shutterbug problems as red-eye, underexposure, and color defects. Once you get the hang of the software, you can also insert new people or backgrounds into photos and add special effects such as halos.

You could take a picture of your spouse showing off her mood rings and within minutes e-mail the shot to your grandson. Or if his parents have a digital camera, you could be looking at a picture of him happily showing off the new gap in his smile from losing his first tooth moments earlier.

Most such digital cameras have a video-out port, so you can show your snapshots on your TV or record them on your VCR. And with a little extra work, you can load them into your personal computer, print them out, post them on a Web page, or e-mail them to family virtually anywhere.

Video Phone Systems

Regardless of how far away you live from your grandchild, you can still see him as often as you want by using the latest in video technology. Obviously, nothing beats being there. But seeing live pictures of him while talking to him from the comfort of your home can be the next best thing.

Among the latest innovations introduced in 1997 are the video phone systems that work off a TV set and those that use a PC. The quality of these video systems doesn't match that of VHS tapes or TV. However, they are more than adequate for long-distance grandparents to get a good look at the grandkids and vice versa. The systems offer reasonably clear images on talking-head close-ups, but any movement in the scene tends to break up the image. Also, you need to scoot up close to the camera for the other party to get a clear look at you.

The more expensive but easier to use system is the TV-based video phone. About the size of a typical cable box, it contains a modem and digital camera. It connects like a VCR to the TV and uses your regular phone line. Once the jacks are plugged in, you're ready to go—assuming, of course, that the person you're attempting to call is equally equipped.

The first two video phone systems to hit the market are C-Phone Corp.'s C-Phone Home and the ViaTV Phone VC100 from 8x8 Inc. They retail for about $550 to $650.

A less expensive, although more complicated, option is the video system for home computers. A camera about the size of a computer mouse is combined with a software package to let people send video by e-mail, post it on an Internet site, or transmit it by standard telephone lines to carry on a video conversation.

Users need a personal computer equipped with a microphone and voice telephone, which are standard in most new home computers. Prices range from $200 for just the camera to $400 for a package with a high-speed modem for transmitting the video and audio. However, you need to be computer-savvy to set it up. If not, you'll probably have to pay someone to install it. The quality of the video depends on the speed of your PC's processor—a Pentium 133 machine is the bare minimum.

Most major brands of home computers are now offering PCs with video phone capability. Among the benefits of this system, a user can share video with others who don't have this video equipment and software. For example, even if you aren't equipped, by downloading certain software, you will have the capability to see video of a grandchild shot by his parents who have a PC-based video system.

Phone

Alexander Graham Bell's invention is a long-distance grand-parent's best friend. Use it!

If money is a problem for your grandchild's parents, give them prepaid phone cards. If you can afford it, get an 800 number so that they'll call you more often. In many cases, the toll-free number doesn't cost anything to install and doesn't require a new line. However, the cost per minute is likely to be higher—as much as double the rate of a long-distance call that you initiate. At least your grandchild's parents can't raise expense as an issue for not calling frequently. (Of course, you don't have to wait for them to call. You can pick up the phone too.)

> **Alisa (Nana) Dollar:** *"We had just come home and there was a message on the answering machine. Our grand-daughter was singing her rendition of 'Twinkle, Twinkle, Little Star.' For Nana and Pop not being around her but three or four times a year, that brought happy tears to our eyes. Little things like that really do mean a lot."*

Susan Newman suggests you plan your calls rather than pick up the phone at your convenience. Know your grandchild's routine, preschool hours, naps, meals, and bedtime. Then call at an appropriate time. If you call at the wrong time, you could face an unsatisfying, hurried conversation.

It doesn't matter how young your grandchild is, it's important for both of you to communicate.

> **Kathy:** *"Even when Chad and Danny were too young to talk, it sure felt good to hear each of them cooing, gur-gling, and babbling some nonsensical sounds. It would make my day. Besides, I got some comfort in knowing that the baby was hearing my voice on a regular basis.*

Every time I'd say a few silly things in the phone, my daughter would point to a photo of me and tell the little one, 'That's your wacky Nana making those stupid sounds.'"

"You should be knowledgeable with what your grandchild is interested in," says Newman. "What's going on in his play group or in preschool? Who are his best friends? You might need to talk to the parents first to find out things about him. Then you can have a fulfilling conversation that relates to him. You'll be able to ask the right questions to get more than a one-word answer.

"You can always find time to call your grandchild. Pick up the phone while you're cooling down from your workout and talk to him or use the cell phone during your commute home. Most young children don't talk on the phone for very long so you should make the most of it."

Fax and Scanners

If you have access to a fax machine, use it to brighten your grandchild's day. Fax a picture, riddle, or comic strip you think he might like. Or fax him a silly drawing and a sweet note just for him. Urge his parents to fax you things that he drew.

Scanners allow you to do virtually anything a fax can do, only better. They can duplicate a color photo, drawing, or text into your computer, allowing you to then post the document or graphic on a Web page or e-mail it to your grandchild.

Videotapes

Who needs Blockbuster? Make your own videos—and get everyone in the family involved. Designate someone in each household to be the family Aaron Spelling and have fun exchanging videos.

If you can afford it, buy your adult child a video camera for the holidays. Then harp on him or her to send you videos of your grandkid. If you don't have a video camera, rent one or borrow one and insist the parents obtain one too.

Make at least one tape solely for your grandchild. Don't stand in front of the camcorder as if you were a graduate of the Ed Sullivan School of Emcees. Loosen up. Sing a song, act goofy like a *Laugh-In* alum, tell a quick story, wrestle with the dog. You're trying to connect with your grandchild. Depending on his age, keep your video segment short and sweet. Remember, his attention span will last about as long as it took Bullwinkle to get into trouble. Speak directly to him just as if he were there in person. But remember: Keep it brief.

Encourage your adult children to make the filming of your grandchild a fun experience for him. It doesn't have to be a Spielberg production. The best shots are those darling moments when he's performing or learning to swim or having fun at a petting zoo.

Share these videos with other family members. Family video exchanges make grandchildren aware of the extended family, of aunts and uncles and cousins. It's a way of keeping everyone connected.

Long-distance grandparents Vic and Lucille Twomey of Illinois have grandchildren in Oregon and Wisconsin. They all stay in touch through a traveling family video. A tape of the grandkids in Oregon is sent to the Wisconsin branch of the family. Members there view the tape and then add their own shots before sending it on to Vic and Lucille in Illinois. After enjoying the video of all their grandkids, the grandparents shoot their segment and ship the tape back to the Oregon family. When the tape is full, the family starts a fresh one. That way, everyone gets to see how the little ones and all the other relatives change and grow.

Tom (Grandpa) Andersen: *"My granddaughter Sara is three and she knows how to run the VCR, so she loves getting videos from us. We live on opposite coasts, so videos are the best way to watch her grow. We miss being there with her, but at least the videos give both of us a chance to stay in closer touch than just the telephone."*

Snail Mail

Children love to receive mail. So send your grandchild notes, postcards, letters, and little gifts on a regular basis.

If you're on the road a lot, pick up a postcard of each place you visit, jot a note about how much you miss him and are thinking about him, and send it off. Traveling nanas and papas often send their grandchildren an album or a special box for the kids to store their collection of postcards.

"You don't have to go anywhere to keep your grandchild 'in mail,'" says Newman. "Send a postcard from a local restaurant, art gallery, or hotel."

Kate (Grandma) Williamson: *"My job requires much traveling. When I'm on the road, I gather the free boxed soaps and shampoos from my hotel rooms and send them to my granddaughter."*

"Grandchildren will look at postcards over and over when they're little," says Newman. "When the children grow up, those cards will have much more meaning to them because it's proof that you've cared about them from the time they were toddlers."

Don't expect to get a written response after every letter or postcard you send. Do it for the joy it brings your grandchild. However, you can boost your chances of receiving return mail by sending him a package of self-addressed stamped envelopes. It makes it easy on his parents to encourage him to respond. If he's a preschooler, ask him to send you a drawing for you to put on the refrigerator or on the wall of your office cubicle.

Send him a stack of prestamped postcards that the post office sells and have him draw you a picture every week. If he's learning to read, keep a stack of the cards for yourself so that you can quickly send him an endearing note. Make sure to print in large, bold letters.

Have a unique signature or picture on the back of every envelope you send him—a smiley face, a rubber stamp or wax impression, or anything that means you and you alone. Take a cue from a nana who uses only purple ink when she writes to her grandchildren or another grandma who uses only green envelopes in mail to her grandson. Even if your grandchild can't read, he can recognize something special from Nana or Papa.

> **Randee (Grammy) Peters:** *"As a long-distance grand-mother, I must share my grandson with three other grandmothers, so I try to make him aware of me by using his sense of smell. Joshua is still too young to read so what I do is scent my letters and postcards to him with my perfume. It's the same perfume I wear whenever I see him. That way, he can equate the scent with me."*

Try to find the time to actually pen a letter. Even if he has trouble reading it, his parents can read it to him. For a nice touch, include in the envelope a little present such as stickers, candy, magnets, a dried flower, trading cards, or even a dollar or two for him to spend.

It really doesn't take much effort to send your grandkid a little gift simply because you love him. Whenever you're at the grocery store or drugstore picking up things for yourself, take a few extra seconds to find something he would enjoy, whether it's a Barney pencil or a Rugrats deck of cards.

Nana Lana: *"I like to surprise my two grandkids, Sammy and Mandy, by sending them little gifts like stickers, money, and books for no reason other than to let them know I'm thinking about them."*

David (Pop-Pop) Pilgrim: *"I'm a glass blower and I don't get to see my kids or grandkids as much as I'd like because we're so far away from each other. On holidays, I make everyone a special figure or ornament. No two are alike. I do the same for their birthdays. It's my way of trying to be there."*

Newman suggests that if your company or volunteer organization has hats, mugs, T-shirts, or other items with the group's logo, send them to your grandchild. It's more than just a reminder that you're thinking about him; it's a way for him to connect with who you are in the work world and what social issues are important to you.

No matter how busy you are, it's well worth the extra time to correspond with your grandchild. The feeling you get when you receive a drawing or note that he made especially for Nana and Papa is second to none. Not only that, but you're nurturing the love of writing and reading—and the love between a grandparent and a grandchild.

If you're really busy, you can still ship special treats to your grandchild on a regular basis. Mail-order houses will send most anything from candies to cookies to flavored popcorn. Many houses will include a brief message from you too.

Long-distance nanas and papas are discovering literary ways to connect with their grandchildren through magazines, book clubs, and newsletters. Consider giving your grandkid a subscription to an age-appropriate publication such as *Humpty Dumpty's Magazine* or *Turtle Magazine for Preschool Kids*. Every time he receives the magazine, it will remind him of you.

If you're at the bookstore, spend a few extra minutes to pick up a book for him. Inscribe it and send it to him.

Sign up for a children's book club that will send him monthly selections. But read the fine print of the club's agreement. Some clubs offer a fixed number of books (usually twenty-four over a year's time), others choose the books for you, and several won't let you cancel unless you've paid for a certain number of books.

> **Harry (Papa) Yeatts:** *"We joined a kids' book club in our granddaughter's name. Once a month or so, she receives a book that we've selected. Her parents always tell her that the new book in the mail came from Nana and Papa. The books let her know we're thinking of her."*

If your grandchild is nearing school age and has a special interest such as whales, tigers, or birds, join a wildlife organization together. Choose one that offers a colorful, graphically pleasing newsletter or publication. It will give you two something to talk about. Or participate in an adopt-an-animal program offered by many zoos and organizations, which also provide newsletters or updates on the animals.

> **Kirk Leiter:** *"I swear I'm on the mailing list of every wildlife organization in America. Many of their pitch letters include stamps, stickers, and cards, so I collect them and pass them on to my grandkids. They love it."*

Photos

Get your face in front of your grandchild as many times as possible. You want more than your fifteen minutes of fame in his eyes. So be shameless.

Put your photo on buttons, magnets, mouse pads, coffee cups, T-shirts, sweatshirts, and aprons for him or his parents to use. You can find computer-photo or video-photo services that offer these products in most malls.

Insert your photo in a toy or holiday ornament specially designed to hold a picture and send it to him. Such items are for sale in many gift catalogs.

Get in the habit of taking photos of yourself doing whatever it is you do—soaking in your hot tub, cross-country skiing, tinkering with your '65 Mustang. Send these photos to your grandchild. In fact, keep a steady stream going. Let him see what an interesting person you are. (You might not want to send those pictures of you at the cross-dressing Halloween party.) Put captions on all the photos; they can provide an early reading experience.

Many experts say that as elders, it's our responsibility to send grandchildren photos of us from the past, so they can get a sense of family history. Oh, sure. Can't you just see sending the little one pictures of Papa with his long, stringy hair and scraggly beard leading a protest rally? Or of Nana go-go dancing in her tube top, hot pants, and shiny white boots? But on the off chance that you can rustle up some not-too-embarrassing snapshots from the past, mail them to him.

Have an informal picture taken of you, put it in a frame, and send it off. Ask his parents not only to display it in a high-traffic area of the house but also to point to it often and refer to you by name. (To ensure the parents' cooperation, threaten to mail your grandkid the photo of his mom when she was being potty-trained.) Make sure all family members, including grandchildren, have a photograph of you to carry around and show others, the way you do with theirs.

Each time you visit your grandchild or he visits you, take plenty of pictures of the two of you together. Put the photos in a little album as a reminder of the great time you both had.

Photography is a two-way street. Badger the parents into taking photos of your grandchild on a regular basis. If you must, buy film for the parents or have them send the undeveloped film to you; heck, buy them a disposable camera. Impress upon them the importance and joy to you of seeing him growing up. If your grandchild is old enough, send him a disposable camera and tell him to take pictures of whatever he wants. Make it easy on everyone by including a return mailer and the money to have the film developed.

> **Jane (Nana) Trebble:** *"We have a tradition of having each family take their own photo at least once a year. Everyone has to be in the same position from year to year so we can all compare the changes over time."*

Audiotapes

To connect with your long-distance infant grandchild, record your favorite nursery rhymes, lullabies, Motown hits, or sorority songs (the cleaned-up versions) and send them to your grandchild's parents to play on their tape recorder. Let your voice become familiar to the baby. When you finally see him, he'll recognize your voice.

Once your grandchild is old enough to carry on a conversation, start an ongoing taped dialogue with him. While you're battling rush hour traffic, keep a tape recorder next to you and record jokes, silly thoughts, old protest songs, a story, whatever you think he'll enjoy. Send it to him with the understanding that he'll record something and return it to you. (Include a self-addressed, stamped mailer.) It probably will be a short reply—but a cherished one. When that tape is filled, save it and start a new one. Your long-distance correspondence can keep going for years—and the tapes will become priceless mementos.

"If your grandchild is in a recital, ask his parents to record it and mail it to you," says Newman. "The tape will allow you to enjoy your grandchild's performance as many times as you like."

> **Joy (Grammy) Tucker:** *"About every other month I record a storybook on tape and then send it, along with the book, to my grandkids. They follow along as Grammy reads it to them. I blow a whistle every time they are supposed to turn the page."*

Internet Bargain Trips

You might be able to see your long-distance grandchild more often than you think—if you're flexible and can take off for a long weekend. It's quite affordable. But there are some catches: You need to live within an easy commute to a major airport to make it worthwhile, and you can't go whenever you want. And, oh yes, you must be wired to the Web.

More than a dozen airlines offer last-minute, Internet-only fares to selected destinations at discounts of up to 75 percent below regular coach. In most cases, available flights are announced on Wednesday night for Saturday departures, returning the next Monday or Tuesday. The airlines will post these specials on their Web sites and some will even e-mail the flight information to subscribers who sign up for this free service.

Airlines use cyberspace to dump unsold seats a few days before departure. For example, each Wednesday, US Airways tantalizes us with rock-bottom, gotta-fly-this-weekend airfares out of Charlotte, North Carolina—the closest big-city airport to our home—to such cities as Dallas for $99 round-trip, Kansas City, $109, and Washington, D.C., $79. But the destinations change every week. You have to pounce on the bargain when the flight is heading to a city near your grandchild. Many times these flights are sold out within a day of being posted on the Net.

For a consolidated list of weekly airfare bargains, check out such sites as Best Fares' Newsdesk (http://www.webflyer.com/@deal/@deal.htm), 1travel.com's Last Minute Deals (http://www.1travel.com), Microsoft Expedia (http://www.expedia.msn.com), Travelocity (http://www.travelocity.com), and Conde Nast's Epicurious site (http://travel.epicurious.com/travel/c_planning/02_airfares/intro.html).

Major hotel chains such as Hilton (http://www.hilton.com) and Radisson (http://www.radisson.com) post their own last-minute weekend bargains, as do American Express (http://www.americanexpress.com) and TravelWeb (http://www.travelweb.com).

You can also find bargains by calling the hotel chain's toll-free number or checking with a discounter such as Hotel Reservations Network (800-964-6835) or Quickbook (800-789-9887).

Be spontaneous. You don't always have to get together only for holidays and special occasions. Take off just because you want to spend time with your grandchild and his parents. And if your spouse can't break away from work, go by yourself.

> **Randee (Grammy) Peters:** *"My business trips sometimes take me through Chicago. When that happens, I try to schedule a layover for a day so I can see Joshua. He lives only thirty minutes from the airport. Once I had a three-hour layover and got a chance to see him because his mom brought him to the airport. It made my week."*

Vacations Together

In many cases, money is the biggest factor preventing grandparents from visiting their grandchildren.

"The family must decide to give a high priority to having grandparents and grandchildren spend as much time as possible together," says Dr. Kornhaber. "This means that the financial re-sources of the family must be pooled to make this happen. Estab-lish a family policy that recognizes the reality of distance and makes a commitment to try to be as close as possible. If the grand-parents can't come to the grandchildren, then send the grand-children—when they're old enough—to Grandma and Grandpa's."

To help bridge the distance gap, Dr. Kornhaber and his wife, Carol, started the Grandparent-Grandchild summer camp at the Sagamore Conference Center (the former Vanderbilt estate) near Raquette, New York, in the Adirondack Mountains. There are no TVs or private phones in the rustic lodge setting—and no parents either. (For further information, see page 205.)

"To reconnect and to reaffirm their vital connection, grand-parents and grandchildren need a place where they can be alone together and share time all their own away from the demands of their everyday lives," says Dr. Kornhaber. "They have a wonderful time."

If you can afford it, why not splurge with a once-in-a-lifetime multigenerational vacation? Go somewhere fascinating together. To learn about special deals for grandparent-grandchildren trips, talk to your travel agent or check out grandparenting Web sites that often highlight such vacations.

Country Cottages, a Florida company specializing in unique accommodations in Britain, offers an incredible program—the Grandparents' Houseparty. A family of four that must include at least one grandparent and one grandchild can fly to Britain, spend a week in their own rented cottage, and have use of a rental car or minivan. In 1998, the cost of this vacation started at $2,896— not per person but for everyone, including round-trip airfare from New York. Prices vary with the season and the number of family members in the group. The company plans on offering similar arrangements in other countries. (For further information, see page 206.)

If you have money to burn, try one of the national or international tours arranged by Grandtravel, which follow itineraries developed by a team of teachers, psychologists, and leisure counselors. According to its Web site, Grandtravel specializes in trips for grandparents and grandchildren that "stimulate curiosity, encourage exploration and discovery, and are fun-filled." Each itinerary is designed to appeal to both generations, with special attention to natural attractions (glaciers, jungles, mountains, canyons), historic sites (native villages, ancient cities, medieval castles), and places of current interest (museums, industries, cultural attractions, beaches). The cost includes hotels, meals, land transportation, tour guides and escorts who are responsible for the academic part of the tour, and cultural activities and games for the grandchildren. (For more information, see page 206.)

If you live within a few hundred miles of your grandchild and aren't able to score any low airfares, you can still find ways to cut travel costs. Try sharing the expenses by having the families meet someplace in the middle at a hotel or resort for a long, fun weekend.

In our case, we live five hundred miles away from our grandsons, so we try to meet somewhere in between. While working on this chapter, we took a long weekend and met the family halfway at Georgia's Stone Mountain Park, where we had a super time together.

Surrogate Grandchildren

Your grandchild is growing and changing so fast, it might be difficult to keep up with him—especially if you don't see him on a regular basis. You don't want to fall victim to a generation gap. But you can keep in touch with his interests, vocabulary, and physical development simply by having contact with children the same age as your long-distance grandchild.

Anna (Nana) Diaz: *"I see my grandson Eddie—he's now three—about every four months. Before our visits, I turn on PBS and watch Sesame Street and Barney (I can only take him in small doses) and a few cartoons so that I'm a 'with it' grandmom in his eyes."*

If you have time, consider acting as a surrogate grandparent, suggests Dr. Kornhaber. At the Foundation for Grandparenting he relates, "We received a letter from an overworked young mother, whose own parents live too far away to help out, who is seeking someone local to grandparent her children. Another such mother wrote asking, 'I have no one to watch my daughter after school. Do you know anyone in this area who would like to be a grandmother to her?' We have even received several letters from children asking if we could find them a grandparent. Talk about heartbreaking!"

Spend time with friends, neighbors, and nearby relatives who have small children. Better yet, become a Big Brother or Big Sister, join the Foster Grandparent Program, become a school volunteer, or work with a children's group at your church or synagogue. Hands-on experience with children will give you a greater understanding of your own grandchild.

Stan (Papa) Twilliger: *"One of my coworkers and good friends married for the second time when he was forty and has a son, Brandon, who is my grandson's age. Because my grandson, Michael, lives so far away, I make it a point of seeing Brandon so I can stay in touch with what four-year-olds are doing."*

Bridge over Troubled Water

Dealing with Blended and Nontraditional Families

When we boomers were growing up, Ozzie and Harriet typified the American family. Dad was the sole breadwinner (forget the fact that Ozzie never seemed to work) and Mom stayed home with the kids. Divorce was almost unheard of.

Today, children are just as likely to live with a single parent, grandparents, stepparents, or nonrelatives as they are to live in the traditional nuclear family. It's not surprising when you look at the following statistics gleaned from the U.S. Census Bureau and the Stepfamily Foundation:

- 66 percent of all marriages and living-together situations involving children end in breakup.
- 50 percent of children will be victims of a divorce before they are eighteen.
- 50 percent of children under the age of thirteen are living with one biological parent and that parent's partner.
- 46 percent of Americans are involved in some form of step relationship.

- Seven million children—one out of ten—live in step-families. By the year 2000, more Americans will be living in stepfamilies than in nuclear families.

Now some boomer nanas and papas are asking such questions as, "What do our former daughter-in-law's children from her new marriage call us?" "Can we take our grandchildren to the ball game without upsetting their stepsiblings?" "Is it okay to feel jealous of our grandson's affection for his stepgrandmother?"

If Your Adult Child Divorces

Divorce has profound repercussions for all family members. Each year, one million children suffer through the split-up of their parents.

Dr. Arthur Kornhaber calls grandparents the "other victims of divorce" because their relationship with their grandchildren can be severely compromised. "Parental divorce can affect grandparents' time with grandchildren, for better or worse," he says. "Helping and supporting the custodial mother may increase the time that grandparents spend with their grandchildren. However, if parents remarry or another set of grandparents takes on a supportive role, grandparents' time with, and access to, their grandchildren may be compromised.

"Parental divorce affects grandparents adversely, especially when they are helpless to do anything about the situation. The matter is complicated even further when grandparents are enmeshed in the divorced couple's problems or when they are emotionally attached to their child's ex-spouse."

Several studies reported that those grandparents whose adult child does not have legal custody of the children have a decreased amount of contact with their grandchildren, especially if they don't live nearby. The same studies show that proximity to the children's custodial parent is a major factor in maintaining a continued grandparent-grandchild relationship.

Dr. Kornhaber says the quality of the relationship of grandparents to the surviving custodial parent (whether or not they are blood related) can determine the degree of grandparent access to the grandchildren. Even if the relationship is less than desired, you can take steps to protect your right to visit your grandchild after the divorce. (The next chapter discusses legal issues.)

If your adult child divorces, you probably will experience some of the same feelings as your grandchild—helplessness over events beyond your control, anger over the situation, anxiety about the future, and sadness over a broken family. Unfortunately, you both must suffer the consequences of the split-up.

Some tips from the experts:

- Focus your attention on your grandchild, not on the parents. During this time of turmoil, she needs your love, support, and understanding more than anyone.
- Be aware that your grandchild may believe she is responsible for the breakup—a feeling that often leads to a poor self-image. Reassure her that she is not the cause; that it's an adult problem that adults must solve.
- Praise her whenever possible and build up her self-esteem. Do your best not to criticize her during this difficult time.
- Encourage her to express her feelings. Give her the opportunity to open up and share her concerns and fears. If you have more than one grandchild in the household, spend time with each one separately so they can talk to you in private.
- Be someone she can count on. Phone or visit regularly no matter what. Be consistent so she knows you will always be there for her.

- Fight the urge to take sides. Your grandchild has only one biological mother and father, so avoid doing or saying something that could hurt her relationship with either parent.
- Be honest with your grandchild—but that doesn't mean you must reveal any or all of the sordid details.
- Remind her repeatedly that she is loved by you and her parents. Tell her that even though her parents are angry at each other, they still love her, and that she doesn't have to stop loving one parent to show affection toward the other.
- Ask her and your adult child how you can help. If they tell you, follow through.
- Find ways to create positive, fun experiences for your grandchild.

Remember, this is the time when your grandchild needs you more than ever, says Barbara Bowman, president of the Erikson Institute. "If you want to have contact with your grandchildren when they grow up, you better be with them when they're young. Swallow your pride if you must. Talk to the parents about how important it is for you not to lose touch with the grandchildren. Even if everyone is furious with one another, the goal is to prevent the children from experiencing harm."

If You Divorce

If you are the one going through a divorce, you can still maintain a close relationship with your grandchild and ease her pain.

"I think this situation involves the same kind of issues as when the parents divorce but to a much lesser extent," says family expert Dr. Gregory Sanders. "The child is not going to be as torn or caught in the middle. Both grandparents need to tell her that their closeness to her won't change, but that some things about the relationship will change, if only slightly. For example, 'You won't come to Grandma and Grandpa's house, but you will see us at our own separate places. We'll keep doing things with you, they just won't be with Grandma and Grandpa together. We may not both be there for holidays, but we will continue to have special times with you.' Her parents can play a role there too by encouraging a closeness in the relationship."

However, the grandparents' breakup can have an adverse affect on the adult children, threatening the stability of the family. "Things will never be the same, but it's up to you to try to keep your relationship with your children and grandchildren as consistent as possible," says Dr. Perry Buffington.

"You need to reassure your grandchild that you'll still be there for her. Do it not only with your words but with your actions. That means you should continue to do the things you used to do with her before the divorce.

"It's not unusual for a divorced grandparent to latch on to their adult children for support. You're looking for validation that you did the right thing. It's only human to do that. But be careful about dumping all your troubles on them and try not to criticize your spouse in front of the family." He also warns of the difficult position you could put your adult children in if you refuse to attend a family function solely because your ex-spouse will be there.

If You Become a Stepgrandparent

A recent study noted that one-third of grandparents interviewed had at least one stepgrandchild. While most grandparents acquire stepgrandchildren when an adult child remarries, other nanas and papas gain stepgrandkids after remarrying following a divorce or a spouse's death. For a child, the remarriage of both of her parents can potentially add four stepgrandparents. And, in that same scenario, if the biological grandparents divorce and remarry . . . well, you get the picture.

Dr. Sanders, of the Department of Child Development and Family Science at North Dakota State University, conducted one of the first studies ever on stepgrandparents. Contrary to the image of the wicked stepfamily, he and researcher Debra Trygstad found some encouraging news for stepgrandparents. In over half the cases, the stepgrandchildren (who were college students at the time of the study) regarded their stepgrandparents in a positive way.

"Most of the stepgrandchildren in this study viewed the stepgrandparent not only as someone they cared for as an individual, but also as someone they respected," says Dr. Sanders. The study found that the stepgrandchildren maintained contact with their stepgrandparents beyond high school; the majority of respondents wanted more contact with their stepgrandparents; and almost half the respondents viewed their relationship with their stepgrandparents as important.

"The stepgrandchildren wanted to see their stepgrandparents more than they had the opportunity to," Dr. Sanders reports. "It's very good that older people can become involved in children's lives and have a positive impact and a positive relationship even without a biological bond."

The Sanders-Trygstad study asked the respondents to answer questions concerning the one stepgrandparent that they saw most often. Among the results:

- 89 percent of the respondents believed that the stepgrandparent deserved respect.
- 67 percent believed that they could learn a lot from their stepgrandparent.
- 50 percent said having a personal relationship with their stepgrandparent was very important.

- 46 percent described their emotional attachment to their stepgrandparent as pleasurable.

"Although not a majority, many saw the relationship as important or extremely important," says Dr. Sanders. "These findings indicate that the relationship goes beyond a formal tie and involves actual interaction and meaning to the family system.

"New stepfamilies might begin to understand the importance of establishing relationships with stepgrandparents, especially when the children are young. The relationship with their stepgrandparents has potential for becoming an additional resource to their family. Children who have stepgrandparents may have an extra set of relatives they can turn to for support."

Dr. Sanders says there are several factors that will determine how easy it will be to develop your relationship with your stepgrandchild. Among the most important:

- The age of the child when you enter her life. The younger she is, the better the chances are that you will forge a close relationship. "You have more time to develop the relationship," says Dr. Sanders. "The older she is, the less likely that you'll be important in her life."
- The child's relationship with her stepparent (your adult child). "If she doesn't get along with her stepparent, then the relationship with her stepgrandparent is not going to be fully developed or seen as important," he says. In the study, the more dissatisfied the child was with the parent's remarriage, the lower he or she rated the importance of the relationship with the stepgrandparents.
- Your relationship with your adult child and his or her new spouse. The biological parent will play a role in establishing the amount of contact that stepgrandparents have with the parent's child. "Also what role the step-

parent expects his or her parents to play with the child is going to have a real impact on how involved the grandparent can be," says Dr. Sanders. If you have a good relationship with the parents, then you likely will have more access and encouragement to develop your own relationship with your stepgrandchild.

Many children may not be quick to adjust to the demands of knowing and accepting a stepparent, stepsiblings, and stepgrandparents, says Dr. Kornhaber. "However, our studies have shown that if stepgrandparents go gently and make themselves available, without asking for any reward or feedback such as verbal declarations of the children's love and respect, the majority can develop significant attachments.

"Stepgrandparents need to relate to members of the extended family and especially the stepgrandchild's caretaker. They must consider the child's other grandparents if they are in the picture. These family arrangements can be fraught with emotional complications that stepgrandparents must identify and deal with if they wish to have smooth relationships with others.

"When the time and circumstances are right, most children can accept a stepgrandparent. After all, the more people a child has to love, the better. When it works, a wonderful bond is formed for life between child and stepgrandparent. But often, it isn't easy to make it work."

He says stepgrandparents can get important clues about how to act by considering and reflecting upon the conditions that made them stepgrandparents in the first place. "For example, if the child has no living grandparents, or lacks a grandparent of the same sex as the stepgrandparent, the stepgrandparent can easily fill that void in the child's heart and soul for a beloved elder. There is no competition. When this works well, it deepens the bond between the biological grandparent and his or her spouse [the stepgrandparent] because they have the love of the child in common."

If the child has living grandparents, the stepgrandparent still can be an important and loving friend to the child, says Dr. Korn-haber. "But the stepgrandparent has to be sensitive—letting the youngster come to the stepgrandparent and being aware of exist-ing [biological] grandparent-grandchild relationships and what is happening in the family. There might be jealousy, envy, and more. The effective stepgrandparent must be a friend to everyone.

"It's best if the stepgrandparent is an available friend, without any needs of his or her own for emotional attachment to the child. The stepgrandparent should try to be as selfless as possible. Emotional maturity is required. You shouldn't try to rush things. Wait in the family wings before entering a child's life.

"Many stepgrandchildren I have interviewed had to deal with profound psychological issues such as dealing with divided loyal-ties, working through the dissolution of the parents' marriage, try-ing to comprehend the circumstances leading to the remarriage of the custodial parent, and trying to make sense of a new family con-figuration. This is a tall order, and the last thing a child needs is to be expected to have an instant relationship with a stepgrandparent. In fact, the child may resent a stepgrandparent at first because the child sees that person as an interloper in a once-secure family life."

Dr. Kornhaber says the watchwords for successful stepgrand-parenting are being patient, offering support, showing love, giv-ing care, and being noncompetitive. "Eventually, if you have stepgrandchildren, you can be a new friend and a new person for them to love. Just be careful to let your new wards come to you. Be there for them when they are ready, and be consistent and re-liable. Remember, don't try to buy their love with gifts. They need the essence of you, and in time you will become an important per-son in their lives. Children have no built-in limit as to the num-ber of people they can love.

"Effective stepgrandparenting is an art, but it can be a source of revelation, great joy, and wonder for those who undertake this role with sensitivity, tenderness, understanding, and compassion."

Dr. Sanders says it's important for you to introduce your family traditions to your stepgrandchildren. "That will help to build the relationship and make you unique. Include your stepgrandchildren in your family history. Let them know what your rituals and traditions are because that can make you special in their eyes."

If you are a new stepgrandparent or will become one soon, don't worry about competing with the biological grandparents, says Dr. Sanders. "There really isn't a need to compete. There's room for both kinds of grandparents. The biological grandparents shouldn't feel threatened by stepgrandparents. The biological grandparents are going to continue to be the most important connection for the grandchild, but that doesn't mean the stepgrandparents can't play an important role and form a positive relationship too. They're not going to come in and take over the grandparenting role, but they can share a role and develop that relationship.

"Kids can't have too many people who care about them and support them."

In homes where there are stepgrandchildren as well as biological grandchildren, it can be tricky to expect the grandparent to treat everyone the same.

"It creates conflicts when kids are treated differently in the same household," Dr. Sanders says. "Say a grandparent is providing child care and the stepgrandchild is treated differently from the biological grandchild. That will create problems. Differences [in how the children are treated] should be discussed openly with the grandchildren and stepgrandchildren to establish the importance of all the relationships. Being open about it will head off some bad feelings that might occur."

Tension appears to be reduced for stepgrandparents who don't have to visit their grandchildren and stepgrandchildren at the same time, he adds.

If you have grandkids and stepgrandkids, Dr. T. Berry Brazelton offers this simple advice: "Do the best you can. The more you can give the stepgrandchild, the better. It's a tenuous relationship at best because you are not that child's grandparent and you feel more committed to your own [biological] grandchildren. You can't help that. So go on and deal with it the best way you can."

If the kids are old enough to understand, feel free to talk to them about your role, he says. "I think you always have to discuss these issues with the kids. They may have the same concerns about you. As for loving or even liking the new grands as you do your own, that is not, realistically, very likely. It's best to let matters take their course."

Dr. Sanders suggests that you work at developing a good relationship with the parents. "The middle generation has a lot of influence over the type of relationship you'll have with your stepgrandchild. Do the parents encourage and support the relationship? What are their expectations of you? Are they willing to find ways to make this a positive experience?"

He says a fairly common concern with new stepgrandparents is what they want the stepgrandkids to call them. "Part of it depends on the age of the children at the time. It's something that needs to be worked out in the families. Calling someone 'Stepgrandparent' is quite a mouthful. I have a stepdaughter and she calls my parents by their first names. From my experience, if the children are quite young when the remarriage takes place, they might be more likely to call the stepgrandparents Grandma and Grandpa."

Some tips from the experts:

- Ask the parents' permission to become involved in your stepgrandchild's life.

- Seek *friendship* first with your stepgrandchild.
- If your biological grandchild has new stepsiblings, spend some time alone with her and offer reassurance. Listen to her fears and concerns.
- Be understanding of your grandchild's feelings about her new living arrangements before you start to build a relationship with your new stepgrandkids.
- Take your time in getting to know your stepgrandchildren. If you push too hard or too fast, you risk getting rejected.
- Enlist your biological grandchild in helping you develop a relationship with your stepgrandkids.

Nontraditional Families

In the days of the Cleavers, Andersons, and Stones, it was odd to have single parenthood by choice, communal living, households headed by nonparents, and same-sex relationships that included children. Today, an increasing number of boomer nanas and papas have adult children who are living in such nontraditional families.

If you don't approve of the family situation, don't let that interfere with your own special relationship with your grandchild, says Dr. Buffington. "Your adult child chose to be in this situation, so it's up to you to accept it.

"In some cases, I've seen grandparents not give as much love and affection to the grandchild just because they are so preoccupied about what the adult child did. The best thing to do is focus on what is in the best interests of the child." He warns that your ill feelings toward your adult child's unique family situation can weaken the bond between the parents and your grandchild.

Because of society's bias, being a part of a nontraditional family is extremely challenging. Don't add to the difficulty. "If you have trouble supporting this kind of lifestyle for your adult child and his or her child, you need to put your own prejudices aside," says Dr. Buffington. "You have a higher issue, a higher ethic to deal with—the needs of a young child. My best advice is: Grandparents, grow up! Make the child your main priority. If you don't, you are incredibly selfish. I can't think of a single, solitary valid reason why a grandparent would not want to be around a grandchild."

If you're still having a problem dealing with this alternative lifestyle, try seeking a professional therapist to help you work it out. Quite frankly, you should be happy that your adult child has been blessed with a child's love. The family would be even more blessed with your love and emotional support.

Interfaith, Interracial, and Intercultural Marriages

If your adult child marries someone of a different race, faith, or culture, you probably have some concerns about the way in which the parents plan to raise your grandchild, especially if it involves beliefs that are far different than yours.

Dr. Buffington believes you should show your grandchild who you are by the way you practice your religion and/or culture. "Children understand that people are different," he says. "There's nothing wrong with families being honest and straightforward about their cultural and religious differences. Just don't do it in a contrived or affected way in an effort to influence the child. But if what you practice and believe has been a part of your life, then don't hide it."

Show off elements of your culture and beliefs during holidays, he says. You can best do this through religious rituals, food, music, and folktales.

In her excellent book *The Essential Grandparent*, Dr. Lillian Carson writes:

Developing children's religious, racial and cultural identity provides them with the building blocks for their identity, the knowledge of who they are. It gives them a sense of belonging to something greater than themselves. When you teach your grandchildren about your unique heritage, you are telling them about yourself. It's a way for them to get to know you. Grandparents have a right to tell their grandchildren who they are, with the parents' permission. When this is done in a nonjudgmental way, you can have a tremendous positive influence.

First of all, face your own feelings and prejudices about the differences. The degree of difficulty this presents depends on deep-seated beliefs. Today we are learning the value of embracing diversity. It enriches our lives. You must proceed with great diplomacy so that you don't offend the parents when transmitting your grandchildren's heritage, by carefully considering what you say and how you say it. By accepting differences, you can bring harmony to the family and nurture mutual respect and love in the midst of ambiguity. . . . This creates a situation that requires great tolerance and a need to appreciate and respect differences. It is a rich learning opportunity.

Nana Lana: *"When we all get together, it's like a mini–United Nations. Jews, Gentiles, Irish, Bahamian, French, Poles. For the holidays, we all bring something for the table. When [grandchildren] Sammy and Mandy get a little older, they will really appreciate their melting-pot heritage."*

Multigenerational Households

Whether your adult child and his or her family move into your home or you move into theirs, you can live harmoniously if you reach an understanding about the living arrangements beforehand.

"It's important, right at the very beginning, to avoid unnecessary misunderstandings and frustrations by clarifying what each one expects of the other," says Nancy Covert, of the Penn State cooperative extension service. "In order to do this, a special time for discussion and decision-making should be set as soon as possible. It isn't always fair to live by 'my rules' or 'your rules.' When two households merge, it's better to clarify what is needed and expected of both by establishing new rules for the group to decide upon."

Hold a family session to iron out issues and avoid potential problems. Include any children who are old enough to contribute to the family discussion. "If the discussion is open, honest, and sensible, young children can feel a real sense of family security, gain self-esteem, and learn how to function as team players," says Covert.

Allowing every member to openly express his or her concerns and suggestions makes for a smoother-running household. "When you plan together, don't expect to agree on everything," Covert says. "You are individuals who have grown up in different eras, with different influences on your lives. These influences often affect how you feel about matters such as money, work, education, food, entertainment, and even religion. Time is needed to work through these differences and come to the best compromise when you cannot agree."

Moving in together can have its benefits, but it also can cause mixed emotions and financial strain, says Jane Mecum, a family agent of the Penn State cooperative extension service. "While it will be great to be around your grandchildren and be an active part of their lives, it can create conflicts. It is important to remember that each adult was living independently before and now each generation will begin to rely on one another."

Some household expenses will be reduced, others increased. Determining who pays for what is an important discussion before any move is made.

"Because there are three generations living together, ground rules will be important," says Mecum. "You may find yourself having more rules now than when you were raising your own children. Little items such as laundry, TV, company, curfews, meal times, discipline, decision-making, and privacy are a few things you will want to talk about. Rules can be changed as the generations blend together. If you are going to share a home with your adult children and grandchildren, you should have a role in important decisions, especially those that affect you directly.

"Constructively solving difficulties that arise when different generations live together will make it easier to share resources, enjoy each other's companionship, and overcome hardships. A clear understanding of roles and responsibilities together with a large dose of respect can make several generations together a functional and happy family unit."

Grandparents Raising Grandkids

Most grandparents raising grandchildren have taken on a labor of love they didn't choose. It chose them. In most cases, a complicated set of circumstances presented these nanas and papas with an unexpected challenge that they accepted—some happily, some reluctantly, some because they had to. At a time in their lives when they expected to be playing more tennis, opening a craft shop, or riding the back roads in their RV, they find themselves enmeshed in diapers, play groups, and PTA. Their free time is now spent battling the court system, social services departments, and health care providers.

They are parenting once again—and it isn't any easier. Less leisure, more laundry; less freedom, more chores; less money, more commotion. And through it all, they wish things had gone better for their kids and feel pangs of guilt because things haven't.

> **Butch Kellett, 47:** *"Starting over at this age, I've learned a lot about patience. It was rough at first [taking in his three-year-old grandson Tyler]."*

> **Kathy Kellett, 43:** *"When you get past the sadness, it's wonderful. We're lucky—not everyone is as excited to raise a grandchild."*

Today more than four million children in the United States live full-time with their grandparents, nearly double the number in 1980, according to the Census Bureau. About one-third of all caregiving grandparents are baby boomers. Countless other grandparents and concerned relatives are dealing with situations in which they wish their grandchildren lived in safer, healthier environments.

"Grandparent caregivers may face legal and social problems," says the American Association of Retired Persons's Grandparent Information Center (GIC). "They may lack support and respite services, affordable housing and/or access to medical services and coverage of medical expenses for the grandchildren.

"These problems are exacerbated by the demands of becoming a parent again, coupled with a more violent environment in which the present generation of children is coming of age. Additionally, some of these grandchildren have special medical or learning needs that may put further financial and emotional strain on the family."

According to the GIC, grandparents are raising their children because of parental substance abuse (44 percent of the cases); child abuse, neglect, or abandonment (28 percent); teenage pregnancy (11 percent); death or divorce of a parent (9 percent); and other reasons including parental unemployment, imprisonment, or illness (8 percent).

Grandparent-headed families come from all socioeconomic levels and ethnic groups. Two-thirds are the maternal grandparents. According to the Census Bureau, 52 percent of the children in grandparent-headed households are under the age of six.

> **Nana on the Net:** *"I love my grandkids, but I wish I could have been just a regular grandparent and spoil them and then send them home."*

This is such a complex issue that it goes beyond the scope of this book. However, according to experts, if you are about to face this situation, consider doing the following:

- Find a support group in your area so you can talk to other grandparents. (Several national organizations are listed in the appendix, starting on page 199.)
- Talk to social agencies and organizations to find out what assistance may be available to you.
- Expect to face many major adjustments in your life that will affect your lifestyle, finances, marriage, career, and friendships.
- Be prepared to improvise in the face of unusual and sometimes difficult situations.
- Understand your legal options, such as temporary or full custody, foster care, guardianship, or adoption. When custody is established by law, grandparents gain rights and benefits not offered with other caregiving arrangements. These benefits include health insurance, social services, government financial assistance, housing, and school enrollment.

Sherry (Grammy) Johnson: *"I was seen as 'interfering' when advocating for my grandchildren's basic needs like baths, sleep, and proper food. It was easier for me just to have them live with me."*

If you already are raising your grandchild, consider these words of wisdom from the experts:

- Don't lie to your grandchild about her parents. Kids are capable of handling the truth. No matter how well-meaning it may seem to fib, lies require high maintenance and they eventually come back to haunt you.
- Keep in mind that the child is not responsible for the situation and should not be put in a position of being blamed or shamed.
- If you're taking on the role of the full-time parent, you must parent. You can't be just the grandparent anymore. That means you have to set the limits, establish the rules, and hand out the discipline.
- Take pride in what you do. You are rescuing a child from a terrible situation and providing her with a loving, stable environment.
- Try to be compassionate, supportive, and flexible to help your grandchild work through the loss of her parents.
- Don't compare this situation to your first parenting experience. Everything is different, including you, the times, the circumstances, and the child.

Nana on the Net: *"I had various grandchildren for days, weeks, and months at a time. I provided almost all of their needs, including paying for their mother's and her boyfriend's rent, bikes, and vehicle. But the drugs and alcohol are fighting me for dominance in my grandchildren's lives."*

"Children raised by grandparents long to have a healthy and loving parent besides their grandparents," says Dr. Kornhaber. "Mature, sensitive grandparents are aware of these dynamics and should defer their own needs to those of the child. It is inherent in the grandparent role to move in and out of being a nurturer, mentor, role model, playmate, and caretaker."

Many grandparents who raise children claim it's another opportunity to enjoy a close relationship. They often report a greater sense of purpose, according to a study conducted by Margaret Jendrek of Miami University in Ohio. In the Grandparent Study, more than 90 percent of the grandparents raising grandchildren stated that doing so has given new meaning to their own lives. Nevertheless, most of them acknowledged having mixed feelings.

"Some grandparents resent the disruption in their lives caused by their grandchildren's needs for time and attention," reports Dr. Kornhaber. "Grandparents raising debilitated grandchildren—such as those with fetal alcohol syndrome, malnourishment, health, behavioral, or learning problems—may resent the extra care required. Others express bitterness that all too often society's institutions do not support their efforts with adequate funding, health care, and social agencies.

"Despite the negative emotions and various problems that may arise, caregiving grandparents feel useful and also derive satisfaction from knowing they are rescuing their grandchildren. Such caregivers in the Grandparent Study said they had increased energy and interest in daily life and noticed an improvement in mood since they started raising their grandchildren. These caregivers report they cope better if they have a family support network."

Another study said grandparents deal with the pressures of raising grandchildren by praying, meditating, having fun with the grandchild, or changing their perspective of the situation so that this burden becomes a mission and a challenge.

> **Nana on the Net:** *"I'm taking action in the interests of my grandchildren. There will be no more bouncing them around. I am prepared to raise them—and to face the results this will have on my adult daughters who'll likely drug themselves into oblivion."*

No matter what kind of nontraditional family your grandchild might live in—single parent, gay parents, interracial marriage, grandparent-headed household—it's not necessarily a bad situation, says Alan Acock, professor and chair of the Department of Human Development and Family Services at Oregon State University. He and David Demo, professor and chair of the Department of Human Development and Family Studies at the University of North Carolina–Greensboro, conducted a study of adolescents. The researchers found that the makeup of a household matters less than does the level of family conflict, income, and education. The lesser the hostility and the higher the household income and education, the better the conditions are for the child. Most important is the quality of time a custodial adult spends with the child.

"Family dynamics are far more important than family composition," says Acock. "You can have a secure, stable, nurturing environment with one parent or two."

The Long and Winding Road

Grandparents' Legal Issues

Powers of Attorney

When we boomers were kids and our parents wanted a break from us, they usually shipped us off to Grandma's house or had Grandma come over to baby-sit while they hopped in their Ford Fairlane and drove on the new interstate to Niagara Falls or Mount Rushmore. Grandma was now in charge and no one outside the family questioned her authority. She didn't have, or need, anything in writing to say she was the boss while the parents were away.

Don't try that today, please. As a devoted grandparent, you need to be legally prepared to care for your grandchild or else you could face serious problems concerning your responsibility for, and relationship with, your grandchild.

If you're baby-sitting for him while his parents are snowboarding in Keystone for the week or if you regularly care for him, you should have legal authorization to make critical decisions on his behalf—especially in case of a medical emergency. Without it, your grandchild may not get the care he deserves.

Because of strict rules and regulations affecting health care today, grandparents need this document. According to the Grandparents Rights Organization, "Other than in life-threatening situations, many doctors and hospitals will refuse a grandparent (or other third party) to secure medical treatment for a minor child unless the adult has a guardianship order from a court or a medical authorization form signed by a parent."

In most cases, you don't have to go to court or even visit an attorney. A simple power of attorney (such as one of the three samples shown in this chapter) signed by the parents will give you the proper authorization. Most states also require that such a form be notarized and/or witnessed.

(The following information on powers of attorney was adapted with permission from the Genesee County [Michigan] Strong Families/Safe Children's Grandparent Guidebook.)

The power of attorney form can be as broad or as specific as the parents wish. For example, it can give you decision-making power just for medical situations. It can also be all-encompassing, granting you the legal right to do things that the parents would do on behalf of your grandchild.

This authorization is good to use if:

- the child's parents are willing and available to sign the forms
- you need to make decisions for the child
- you need this power for more than a short time
- you and the child's parents want them to be able to take back the power quickly at a later time
- you want the parents to spell out the specific powers and decision-making abilities that they are granting you
- you don't want the court involved

Depending on the state, a parental power of attorney is good for only a certain length of time, such as six months or a year. If you and the parents want it to be for a shorter time, you should say so on the form. For a longer period of time, the parents will have to fill out another power of attorney when the previous one expires.

The power of attorney can be changed or taken away at any time by the parents by signing another document saying they revoke the powers they had given you.

If you're baby-sitting for a specific period of time or watch your grandchild regularly, it's wise to have a special power of attorney for medical care. Here is a sample:

SPECIAL POWER OF ATTORNEY FOR MEDICAL CARE

We/I, [name of parent(s)], hereby name [your name and/or your spouse's] as our/my attorney in fact (hereinafter "our/my agent"), and grant to our/my agent the limited authority to care for our/my child, [name of child], as follows:

1. We/I grant to our/my agent the authority to consent to all medical care necessary to our/my child's health and well-being during the time our/my child is in the care of our/my agent.

2. This power includes, and is expressly limited to, the following: the power to consent to all medical, dental, and/or hospital care, treatment, and procedures.

3. [If there are more specific purposes for allowing the power, write it here: _____.]

4. The provisions in this document are to be construed with this express purpose in mind.

This power shall expire and all authority thereunder is revoked on [date of expiration].

Date: _____

Signature(s) of Parent(s): _____.

Print/Type Name & Address:

_____

_____

_____

Phone: _____

On [date], [name of parent(s)], who are/is known by me, appeared before me to execute this document, and have/has acknowledged this to be their/his/her free act and deed.

_____ Notary Public,

_____ County,

My Commission Expires: _____

A general power of attorney is the same kind of permission, but it gives you, as the grandparent, the right to do almost anything a parent could do concerning the child's health, support, care, and well-being. (It does not grant standing in a custody suit.) Here is a sample:

GENERAL POWER OF ATTORNEY
CONSENT FOR CARE OF MY CHILD

We/I, [name of parent(s)], hereby name [your name and/or your spouse's] as our/my attorney in fact (hereinafter "our/my agent"), and grant to our/my agent the authority to care for our/my child, [child's name], as follows:

1. It is understood that [child's name] shall remain in the care of our/my agent until [date of termination].

2. We/I grant to our/my agent the power and authority to do all things necessary to ensure the safety and well-being of our/my child while in the care of our/my agent. This power includes [cross out and initial or delete any that do not apply] the power to consent to all medical, psychological, dental, and/or hospital care, treatment, and procedures; consent to receive, deliver, or pay money and property due to our/my child; receipt of all confidential information or records concerning our/my child; enrollment of our/my child in any school, place of worship, club, etc. This delegation does not include the power to consent to adoption of this child.

3. The express purpose of this power is to allow the agent to do all things necessary to ensure the safe and efficient care of our/my child, and to do all things necessary for his/her care.

4. [If there are further specific purposes, write them here]:

_____

5. All provisions contained herein are to be interpreted with this/those express purpose(s) in mind.

This power shall expire and all authority thereunder is revoked on [date of expiration].

Date: _____

Signature(s) of Parent(s): _____

Print/Type Name & Address:

_____

_____

_____

Phone: _____

On [date], [name of parent(s)], who are/is known by me, appeared before me to execute this document, and have/has acknowledged this to be their/his/her free act and deed.

_____ Notary Public,

_____ County,

My Commission Expires: _____

In cases when you're involved in long-term care for your grandchild, you might need written authorization from the parents to deal with school issues involving him—from teacher conferences to allowing him to go on a field trip.

Many agencies and offices have a legal duty to keep information about children private. They are not allowed to release information to anyone other than a parent, unless the parent signs a paper saying this is okay. This is an important protection for children, but it may keep you from talking to your grandkid's teachers or seeing his school records.

You can receive this education-related information for as long as the form allows, or until the parent takes away your permission. Here is a sample:

RELEASE OF EDUCATION-RELATED INFORMATION

We/I [name of parent(s)] hereby authorize the release of all information, confidential and otherwise, written or verbal, pertaining to our/my child, [name of child], to [your name and/or your spouse's]. We/I authorize [your name and/or your spouse's] to request and receive any and all information from any school, teacher, education administrator, scholastic or educational records, or any other educational source regarding our/my child's schooling, education, educational behavior, grades, homework, schoolwork, learning ability or disabilities, psychological or emotional treatment or development, and all information related to schooling or education whether or not subject to heightened privacy standards. This release includes [cross out and initial or delete the items that don't apply] permission to attend and participate in school activities for or with our/my child, such as field trips, parent-teacher conferences, parents' school associations of any kind, and the like. We/I release all agencies, schools, educational institutions, boards, teachers, administrators, persons, offices, and the like from any liability on account of any disclosure authorized by this release. A photocopy of this release shall be acceptable as an original. This release shall expire on [date of expiration] or upon our/my written revocation, whichever is sooner.

Date: _____

Signature(s) of Parent(s): _____

Print/Type Address: _____

_____

_____

_____

Phone: _____

_____ / _____
Child's Date of Birth and Social Security #

Signature of Witness: _____

With all of these cases, keep the completed original form in a safe place. But first make copies and use them whenever possible. If there is more than one child involved, all their names can go on the same power of attorney form or you can use a separate form for each child. If you and your spouse are going to be agents, both your names must be on the form.

These forms must be signed by all custodial parents or guardians. If more than one person has physical and legal custody, they all must sign. In most states, the parents must sign in front of a notary public. If both parents will not be able to sign in front of the same notary at the same time, you should get a separate power of attorney from each custodial parent. Because laws differ from state to state, it's best to contact your personal attorney if you have any questions concerning a power of attorney.

Grandparent Visitation Rights

It's sad, but an increasing number of grandparents are relying on mediators or waging court battles simply for the right to spend time with their own grandchildren. For them, multigenerational family harmony is something that can only be experienced on old reruns of *The Waltons*.

Most such visitation disputes occur when the grandparents' former son-in-law or daughter-in-law has custody of the children after a bitter divorce or the tragic death of a parent. For whatever reason, the custodial parent denies the grandparents access to the grandchildren. Fortunately, state laws now provide grandparents the opportunity to seek reasonable visitation rights.

Although no one knows how many such court cases are filed in the United States today, noted grandparents' rights advocate Richard Victor says the number of cases his law firm handles has increased tenfold since 1979. Because of the enormity of the problem, he founded the nonprofit Grandparents Rights Organization (GRO). It advocates laws that protect the grandparent-grandchild relationship and provides information to grandparents, legislators, and media and assists support groups.

Says Victor, GRO executive director and an attorney in Birmingham, Michigan, "When I got involved in this issue in 1978, there were no laws [concerning grandparents' rights]. It wasn't because the legislators thought grandparents shouldn't have rights; it was because nobody thought such laws were necessary. Well, they were. We helped get laws passed in all fifty states."

However, the legal rights of grandparents differ widely from one state to another. Efforts to establish a uniform law that applies nationwide so far have failed.

Nevertheless, the laws have helped reunite an untold number of grandchildren with their grandparents. Reports Dr. Arthur Kornhaber of the Foundation for Grandparenting, "Hundreds of grandchildren entangled in these interfamily disputes told us they couldn't reveal their true feelings about their love for their grandparents to their parents. They were forced to go emotionally underground. Many grandchildren dreamed of reuniting with their grandparents when they became older. This wish was strongest when children were very close to their grandparents at a young age. Fortunately, for many this wish is now coming true."

Most states highly encourage mediation or alternative dispute resolution. "If the visitation issue can't be resolved there, then the judge makes the ultimate decision," says Dr. Kornhaber. "You wish that wasn't the case, but grandparents need the court as an option because sometimes that's the only way to get people to the table to talk."

With the increasing number of boomer grandparents, the grandparents' rights movement is gaining strength. According to Victor, "Grandparents today are different than those in decades past. Now that baby boomers are becoming grandparents, they won't allow the emotional abuse of children to occur or continue without speaking up.

"Many grandparent visitation denials occur following divorce when the custodial parent chooses not to associate with his or her former in-laws. This decision has the effect of amputating children from their grandparents. Parents must understand that even though former in-laws are no longer members of that family, those adults are still—and always will be—family to the children.

"Imagine the agony a child feels when his parents and grandparents—adults whom he loves—don't like each other. This agony is intensified when he finds himself the 'prize' to be won or lost in legal disputes. Parents need to remember this, and realize that their children have rights which should not be denied unless it is in their best interests to do so.

"Studies have shown that multigenerational contact between children and their grandparents—and even great-grandparents— provides a special unconditional love and nurturing which is healthy for children. If death takes a grandparent from a grandchild, that's a tragedy. But if family bickering and vindictiveness deny a child the love of a grandparent, that's a shame."

Marilyn Daniels, Ph.D., conducted for the GRO one of the first-ever studies of the grandparents' rights issue.

"The general tenor of the grandparents' responses were of people who had been through a terrible ordeal," she says. "One grandmother described holding her granddaughter one and only one time—in the hospital, the day of her birth. Another was haunted by the memory of her grandchild's face. She said she was 'having a hard time forgetting her, although I've been told to forget her.'

"As I studied the survey responses, I was amazed by the apparent senselessness of the withholders' actions. In many cases, it seemed that parents withheld the children with little or no provocation. I can think of few other examples in the field of family problems in which one category of persons is free to inflict misery on another so effortlessly and without social sanction."

According to the study, there is no typical kind of grandparent or custodial parent whose personal characteristics lead to a visitation dispute. "It can happen to any grandparent," Dr. Daniels warns.

In disputes over grandparent access to children, 50 percent of the cases involve former daughters-in-law or former sons-in-law (sometimes in collusion with their new partners); 32 percent involve "intact" families where the grandchild's parents are married; 9 percent involve an out-of-wedlock birth; 7 percent involve the death of the grandparents' own son or daughter; and 2 percent involve the adoption or foster care of the grandchild. Of the parents who deny their children access to grandparents, an overwhelming 81 percent are women (most likely because of the higher incidence of divorced mothers gaining custody).

"I was startled to find that although most of the grandparents knew the whereabouts of their grandchildren, some seemed to know little about the withholding parent, and many knew little about the withholding parent's new spouse or live-in lover," says Dr. Daniels.

"Many grandparents didn't know such basic information as the person's religion, occupation, education, times married, or total number of children. It's no wonder that so many grandparents worry about the well-being of their grandchildren. They find it maddening to know so little about these people who are living with, influencing, and acting as parents to their grandchildren. These other adults who have access to the children are virtual strangers to the grandparents."

The GRO survey found that 42 percent of the grandparents thought the withholding parents acted entirely on their own. Of the 44 percent who thought the parents were swayed by others, nearly two-thirds identified "the other grandparents" as influencing the withholder.

Withholders often make visiting difficult or embarrassing for grandparents. "This is an attempt to discourage contact without actually forbidding it," says Dr. Daniels. "Many of the grandparents in the study reported on how uncomfortable they felt when they attempted to visit."

Deliberate misunderstandings about the timing of the grandparents' visits are common. "Grandparents were left waiting in their cars or on porches during times of appointed visits," she reports.

"Some grandparents were not invited to sit down, even when they were allowed inside the withholder's house. Sadly, when visits were allowed, the parents often exerted some kind of negative pressure on the situation, making the children feel strange about being friendly toward their grandparents. In a number of cases, these awkward feelings were later used by the parents as evidence that the children 'didn't want to see,' or 'didn't really like,' or 'didn't really know' the grandparents."

Obviously, the best way to avoid such a heart-wrenching situation is to work at keeping a good relationship with your adult child and his or her spouse. The next best thing is to legally protect your right and your grandchild's right to see each other.

> **Gramma Kay:** *"When our son divorced, I was devastated. I thought I'd never see [her grandson] Trevor again. But I made a determined effort to be friendly with his ex-wife even though we never had a really good relationship. She understands that Trevor deserves to see his gramma."*

If your child is in the midst of a divorce, encourage him or her to add grandparent visitation rights in the decree. Divorcing parents can prevent later intergenerational conflict by including in their separation agreement a provision stating specifically that both sets of grandparents will have visitation rights.

If it's too late for that and visitation rights were not included in the decree, you can apply to the local court with appropriate jurisdiction for the right to visit with an unmarried minor child. However, the courts must consider whether grandparents' visitation is in the best interest of the child.

In most states, if the custodial parent has remarried and the new spouse has adopted your grandchild, you still have a right to petition the court for visitation rights with him.

You'll have a much tougher time arguing your case if both the mother and father in an intact family don't want you visiting, warns Victor. "There are challenges saying the constitutional rights of parents cannot be infringed by courts forcing them to grant grandparent visitation."

In extreme cases, some grandparents are reluctant to seek outside help for fear the parents will retaliate by barring them from visiting their grandchildren, says Dr. Kornhaber. "If little Harry's parents are smoking God-knows-what all day and Grandma wants to blow the whistle to the authorities, the parents can say, 'Call the cops, Grandma, and you'll never see Harry again.' However, the court could remove the child from the home in such a case, opening up other legal access for Grandma."

If you are denied access to your grandchildren for whatever reason, Victor offers these suggestions:

- Find alternative ways to continue the relationship. "Write letters and call," advises Victor. "Let the grandchildren know you're part of their support network. And never, never make them feel they have an emotional conflict of interest. Even if you have to bite your tongue when you say something nice about the custodial parent, do it because you're doing it for the good of the children."
- Don't be too aggressive. If the custodial parent remarries, give him or her plenty of time to make the new marriage

work. "Such family transitions are usually difficult for young children, who may be torn by loyalty to the divorced or deceased parent."

- Join or form a self-help support group in your area to exchange information, discuss problems, and promote local, state, and national laws.

- Before consulting an attorney, try to diffuse the situation by talking to the custodial parent. Call, write, or arrange a meeting with the parent to find out the motive for denying access to the grandchildren. "More often than not, visitation is not being denied because the parent thinks contact with the grandparents will be harmful for the children. Instead, the parent fears that the grandparents will talk to the children about him or her in an adverse way."

- Agree with the parent to recognize that the best interests of the children should be put first. "Make that the basis for the starting point of any communication."

- Avoid confrontational and accusatory statements. "You each have a right to think, feel, and believe in your own way."

- If necessary, use a third party such as a social worker, family counselor, or mediator. "Neutral mediators can help adults talk out and resolve family problems that brought about the breakup which resulted in the denial of access to the grandchildren. Reconciliation is preferable to litigation for everyone concerned—especially the children."

- If this informal mediation fails, consider litigation. "Turn to this as a last resort only if you feel it would be in the children's best interest."

- Consult with an attorney who specializes in family law, preferably one with experience in third-party (other than parental) visitation rights. "Often local bar associations will have listings for such attorneys through lawyer referral services."

- Present the attorney with documented evidence and lists of witnesses to support your contention that it's in the "best interests of the children"—the legal standard in most states—for them to see you. Your case is strengthened if you can show a consistent, caring relationship existed between you and the children in the past.

Papa on the Net: *"What we have been through to get to see our grandchildren, I wouldn't wish on anyone. The negative energy of battling in court—of dealing with lies, half-truths, and false accusations, not to mention legal fees—saps you of your inner strength. But was it worth it? Yes, because now we get to see our grandchildren."*

If you do go to court, the laws don't give you an absolute or unqualified right to visitation, says attorney Daniel Clement, who practices marital and family law in New York and New Jersey. The burden is on the grandparent to show that he or she has "standing" to seek visitation and that the visitation is in the best interest of the child.

But each state has slightly different interpretations and standards on which courts base their decisions. In a recent overview of grandparent visitation laws, Clement wrote, in part:

There are no hard and fast rules to determine when circumstances exist so as to require courts . . . to grant a grandparent visitation with their grandchildren. Every case must be determined upon its own facts and circumstances.

165

The nature and extent of the grandparent-grandchild relationship is the focus of the court's inquiry. The longer and stronger the bond between grandparent and grandchild, the greater the likelihood a court would confer visitation rights on a grandparent. Conversely, the more superficial the relationship, the less likely visitation rights will be conferred.

Another factor examined by the court is the basis of the parent's objection to permitting the grandparent to have visitation with the child. Mere animosity between the grandparent and parent may be an insufficient basis to deny a grandparent visitation. However, where a court finds that the grandparent's relationship with the parent and/or the child is dysfunctional, visitation may be denied.

In establishing the relationship with the grandchild, the New York Court of Appeals (New York's highest court) had said it is not sufficient that the grandparents allege love and affection for the grandchild. They must establish a sufficient existing relationship with their grandchild, or in cases where that has been frustrated by the parents, a sufficient effort to establish one so that the Court perceives it as one deserving the Court's intervention. If the grandparents have done nothing to foster a relationship or demonstrate their attachment to the grandchild, despite opportunities to do so, then they will be unable to establish that conditions exist where "equity would see fit to intervene." The Court continued to point out, "The evidence necessary will vary in each case but what is required of the grandparents must always be measured against what they could reasonably have done under the circumstances." Where, for instance, a grandfather made no attempt to have contact with his five-year-old granddaughter from the time she was two weeks old, and had alienated his own children, the grandfather failed to establish conditions where equity would see fit to intervene. Similarly, where the Court found the grandparents' effort to establish a relationship with the grandchild to be superficial or contrived, it has refused to use its equitable powers to order visitation.

On the other hand, where a grandfather demonstrated a concerted effort to establish a relationship with his granddaughter immediately upon learning of her birth, by sending gifts, writing letters, making telephone calls and seeking the aid of third party intermediaries, all to no avail, the Court found that he did all he could do under the circumstances to establish a relationship with his granddaughter. While the Court noted that the grandfather did not have an existing relationship with the grandchild, it took notice of the grandfather's efforts to establish the relationship and found that he had standing to seek visitation.

Therefore, in the absence of an existing grandparent-grandchild relationship, courts will measure what grandparents did to establish a relationship against what they could reasonably have done under the circumstances. No court will intervene where the grandparents have made no effort to establish a relationship with the grandchild.

Assuming that the grandparents established standing to seek visitation, the court will determine if the visitation is in the best interest of the child. . . . The court will undertake an exhaustive examination of all the relevant facts and circumstances, which will include the grandparents' interpersonal relationships, and their relationships with their own children, particularly the grandchild's parents.

In one extreme case, it was found not to be in a child's best interest to have visitation with a grandmother who urged the mother to give the child up for adoption and, when the mother refused to do so, barred the mother and child from living in her house. In another extreme case, the court left it up to the grandchildren to decide if they wanted to have visitation with the grandparents, who denounced them when [the grandchildren] revealed that they had been sexually abused by their parents.

In a more typical case, the grandchildren's parents both objected to the maternal grandparents having visitation with their children since the relationship between parents and grandparents deteriorated. As the Court found, family get-togethers were subject to "stress, tension and uncertainty" due to the grandfather's desire to be controlling and make demeaning comments to the parents and grandchildren. Making matters worse, the grandfather refused to accept responsibility for the deterioration of the family's relationship. For this reason, the Court found that it was not in the grandchildren's interests to have visitation with their grandparents.

Undoubtedly, the fact that the children in the foregoing case came from an intact family and that both parents objected to the visitation with the grandparents weighed heavily in the Court's finding. For, as the Court noted, "As fit parents, respondents have the right to choose with whom their children associate. . . . The record establishes that respondents acted reasonably on the basis of legitimate concerns for the welfare of their family."

While the existing law, as written, is applicable to grandparents seeking visitation with grandchildren of intact families (where the grandchild's parents are not divorced and are both alive), a number of courts have questioned the constitutionality of this application. It is claimed that such application constitutes an invasion upon the parents' right to privacy concerning the manner in which they raise their children. This issue remains unsettled.

In summary, in order to have and maintain visitation with a grandchild, the grandparent should attempt to build a meaningful relationship with the child as soon as possible. If the grandparent's efforts to have visitation are rebuffed by the child's parent, the grandparent should document his or her attempted contacts and continue to send birthday and holiday cards and presents to the grandchild and take other reasonable steps to maintain the relationship with the grandchild. If visitation cannot be amicably arranged, the grandparent should consult with an attorney for an explanation of his or her rights and the local laws regarding visitation.

Nana on the Net: *"If you care enough about your grandchildren, you'll fight to the death for them. If it means spending some of your profit sharing, so be it."*

Under most state laws:

- If a prior divorce action had been filed by the parents, the grandparent must file a request for visitation with the judge who granted the divorce.
- If the case involves the death of a parent, then the grandparent must file a request for visitation in the state and county where the grandchild resides.
- If the case involves an out-of-wedlock child, the grandparent must file a request for visitation in the state and county where the parent raising the child resides.

Since legislation varies from state to state, even if you win your case in one state, you may have to start all over again if your grandchild moves to another state.

Among the court's criteria for a child's best interest:

- love, affection, and other emotional ties that exist between the child and grandparent
- the ability of the grandparent to provide the child proper care during visits
- the relationship between the grandparent and child prior to filing the petition
- the moral fitness of the grandparent
- the mental and physical health of the grandparent
- the reasonable preference of the child if the court deems him or her old enough
- any evidence that the grandparent tried to adversely affect the child's relationship with the parents
- any history of domestic violence or abuse involving the grandparent

Grandparent visitation rights are not intended or designed to supersede parental authority. But sometimes in desperate situations, it might be necessary to consider gaining custody of your grandchild. Consult an attorney and be ready to face a painful and emotional ordeal.

However, if you believe there is a threat to your grandchild's safety, experts advise that you must step in immediately to protect him. If there is evidence that he is being physically or emotionally abused, contact the department of social services in the state where he lives.

At least now we have laws recognizing the integrity and importance of the grandparent-grandchild bond, giving nanas and papas an opportunity to love and nurture grandchildren. For those of you who must go through mediation or a court battle, hang tough and stay positive. Advises Dr. Kornhaber, "Keep your family as intact as possible, strive for healing, and never give up. Today, the Foundation for Grandparenting receives phone calls and letters from grandparents and grandchildren who have reunited and want to share their joy with others. Interestingly, many [custodial and once-adversarial] parents are also happy about this reunion. This confirms that people are capable of growing and changing for the better."

There's Enough to Go Around

Sharing Your Financial Assets

As a grandparent, perhaps you should think about sharing more than your love. If you haven't already, consider sharing some of your wealth. Sure, we boomers have been told that we're overextended and haven't stashed enough for retirement. Nevertheless, now is the time to help provide for our grandchildren's financial needs and future by giving them—and perhaps their parents—cash gifts, by establishing trusts, and/or leaving them property in our wills.

Dr. Arthur Kornhaber, of the Foundation for Grandparenting, recommends that you call a family conference to discuss the funding of your grandchildren's educational and recreational activities. "With costs continually rising, parents today may not have the resources to do this alone," he says. "Family teamwork may be necessary."

Maybe the young family needs your help paying for day care, preschool, medical bills, or gymnastics lessons. If you've got the dough, show them the money. Here's your chance to play John Beresford Tipton on a much more affordable—and meaningful—scale. You and your spouse each can give up to $10,000 a year tax-free to each grandchild (or to anyone else you wish, like your personal trainer or aromatherapist—but why waste it on them?).

Says Barbara Bowman of the Erikson Institute, "The conventional wisdom of a generation ago was that the kids should be able to make it on their own. Today young people are finding that it is not as easy to make it on their own as they had anticipated. It is important for grandparents to provide for some kind of resources.

"One issue is: 'If I give you money, you have to spend it my way.' That's not a very good way to support your adult children. If you can afford to give it, then give it. Assume your children will use it wisely or that they will use it for the specific purpose for which they need the money. To offer them money and tell them how to spend it deprives them of the opportunity to grow up."

Money can help take the pressure off them and make them better parents to your grandchildren, Bowman adds.

"Some grandparents give the money to the parents, believing the parents probably know what's best to do with it," says noted certified financial planner Jeff Wallem. "Often the parents are the ones who need the help. But then there's the issue of loss of control of your money. It depends on the relationship and trust you have with your adult children."

Even though your financial worth is a few zeroes shy of Ted Turner's, you still can start an education fund for your grandchild. Many states offer an affordable monthly installment program that locks in future college tuition fees at today's rates. You might want to contribute to such a plan so that if your grandchild attends a state school years from now, her tuition is covered. (If she chooses to go out of state or to The Mahareshi School of Levitation, you can get your money back.) Many public or private schools are establishing their own tax-exempt tuition programs. Under a new law enacted in 1998, withdrawal of funds from qualified installment programs may be used for room and board as well as for tuition, fees, books, supplies, and required equipment.

The Education IRA, which was created in 1998, lets grandparents (and parents too) save for a child's college education with tax-free distributions for qualifying educational expenses. You can make annual nondeductible contributions of up to $500 per student until she turns age eighteen. Any earnings over the years build up tax free. Withdrawals to pay qualified higher education expenses of the child are tax free. Contributions to Education IRAs don't count toward your $2,000 yearly contribution limit on your own IRA, so you can save for her education and still maximize your own retirement savings. "Education IRAs may become even more advantageous in future years if Congress moves ahead with plans to increase the annual contribution limit," says Wallem.

You might consider a modest investment strategy for your grandchild. Let's say you put one hundred dollars a month away for her for eighteen years—a total of $21,600. At a 10 percent rate of return, the fund will have grown to $60,056 (not factoring any deductions for taxes or transaction expenses). At three percent inflation, that sum would be the equivalent of $36,651 in today's dollars.

> **Tom (Grandpa) Andersen:** *"I put two dollars a day away for my granddaughter Sara. I increase that total by twenty-five cents a year. It's all invested so that when she graduates high school, she'll have enough for college."*

Wallem, of Wallem Associates of Rockford, Illinois, says one of the easiest and most popular ways to help your grandchild with an education fund is to set up a custodial account under the Uniform Gift to Minors Act (UGMA). This lets you create an investment account for your grandchild without the hassles and expense of setting up a trust. Under UGMA, you can give her securities, cash, life insurance, and annuities.

For example, you can transfer or buy shares in a mutual fund in the name of an adult who acts as custodian. "That's very simple, very easy," Wallem says. "The only problem is that the child will have control of the money when she reaches the age of majority, which is eighteen in most states. That could be a hang-up. The grandparent says, 'I want the money to go for college' and the eighteen-year-old says, 'I want it to go toward a red Corvette.'

"If there's a good relationship between the teenager and grandparent, the teen likely will listen to the grandparent who says, 'I gave you this money for college and that's what I want you to use it for.' Hopefully the moral persuasion will work. But if the teen says, 'I am of age so give me the money,' you have to do it." (Can you imagine what you would have done with $60K back when you turned eighteen?)

To avoid the possibility of bankrolling a teenage spendthrift, some grandparents have opened a savings account or bought EE bonds. But Wallem says mutual funds historically bring much higher returns. "The problem with a bank savings account is that, although it is insured, it is paying about what the inflation rate is, and a savings bond yield is also low. If the child has quite a few years before using that money [for college], an aggressive growth mutual fund makes a lot of sense. Generally, though, the higher the potential return, the higher the potential risk."

There are some possible tax consequences to the parents, however. The first $650 of unearned income from the child's investment is tax free. The next $650 of interest income will be taxed at the child's rate if the child is under age fourteen. Any additional unearned income is taxed at the parents' rate until the child turns fourteen when, thereafter, the income is taxed at the lower marginal rate.

"If you want to add to your grandchild's mutual fund, do it on a frequent basis, like monthly, rather than all at once at the end of the year," Wallem suggests. You could have a slightly better return on your investment that way.

"Also, there is a technique called dollar cost averaging which has a psychological aspect to it. If you put money in on a regular basis, it's easier to accept those times when the market goes down because you are buying shares cheaper. If you put in $2,000 once a year and then the market goes down, you feel awful. But if you invest $175 a month there won't be such an adverse psychological impact.

"Even if you have a modest net worth and aren't in a position to give very much, yet you want to give something, the UGMA approach might be right for you. You probably don't want, or need, to go through the legal expense of creating a trust."

Make sure that you read all the information, including the prospectus, about any new investment and fully understand what you're buying, adds Wallem.

If you can, set up a fund now; don't wait until you're as crotchety as Grandpa Amos McCoy. "If you give the money now and not later, it will have more time to grow and compound," says Wallem. "Having an additional ten to fifteen years for that money to grow can make a huge difference as opposed to giving the same amount of money just when your grandchild gets ready for college.

"There's also a learning dimension to this. Our educational system does a poor job of preparing young people to manage their own money when they are adults," he says. One way to help prepare your grandchild for handling money is to set up a mutual fund that includes some stock such as Disney or Nintendo that would be of specific interest to her.

"Maybe by the time she's ten years old, she will be interested enough to check the paper and learn the basics of investing. It's an abstract concept for a young person. But if you can turn her into a saver and an investor at a young age, she might save or invest wisely when she starts earning her own money. She's less likely to spend it all. You will have done that child a huge favor."

For their grandchildren, some boomer grandparents are setting up mutual funds that have kid appeal or a social bent, such as an environmental focus. These funds, which guarantee the principal, are designed for parents and grandparents to save for a child's future. The fund material is even written for kids to understand.

Often, though, these kinds of specific funds aren't as diversified as other more traditional growth funds are. "Depending on your situation, you might consider buying a good, broadly diversified mutual fund and a few shares of stocks you think your grandchild will, when she's a little older, enjoy following," says Wallem.

You definitely should consider your own tax situation before giving a financial gift to anyone, he adds. "Let's say you owned some shares of Microsoft that you bought at five dollars and it's now worth one hundred dollars. You can gift those shares of stock to your grandchild without having to pay taxes on the gain in the shares. However, your grandchild will have to pay any capital gains taxes whenever the stock is sold because your basis becomes your grandchild's basis."

Under the Uniform Transfers to Minors Act (UTMA), you can transfer any property interests to your grandchild, such as real estate, partnership interests, patents, royalty interests, and intellectual property. Like an UGMA account, a UTMA gift is put in the name of a custodial adult on behalf of the minor.

If you want total control of how your gift money is spent, you might want to set up a trust that can be funded by existing money, life insurance policy proceeds, or other property. The beauty of a trust is that you dictate the terms. A basic trust will allow your grandchild to draw a certain amount of funds at certain times for certain reasons—all according to the terms you drew up in the trust. That way, when your grandchild reaches a certain age, she can't blow your money investing in plastic pink flamingoes or a new line of Nehru jackets. The trust can be as simple or as complex as you want.

"There are different types of trusts with different features to them," says Wallem. "You should have one drafted by an attorney. A trust is usually driven by the tax situation of the person giving the money more so than of those who benefit from it."

Even if you're not ready for trusts, UGMAs, and UTMAs, you may have assets and valuable personal items that you want to give directly to your grandchildren at some future time. If so, include those items in your will. (You do have one, don't you?) Putting your wishes down in writing helps ensure that your mint condition turquoise Elvis Pez dispenser and your cherished Ginny Doll collection will go directly to your grandkids.

With banks, brokerage houses, insurance companies, and mutual fund companies all competing for your business with a variety of financial products, gifts, and services, where do you go? Before you do anything, says Wallem, consult with a professional, such as a certified financial planner. "The good CFP will act as the old family doctor. Like the general practitioner, the CFP determines your situation, walks you through the alternatives, and then, if need be, refers you to a good specialist. For example, if it's determined that you have a complex situation, the CFP might put you in contact with a trust attorney or an estate planning attorney. The CFP looks at the broad picture and coordinates the specialists who will best serve you in your situation. Personal chemistry between you and the CFP is important because you need to feel comfortable with someone who is suggesting to you where to invest your money."

Another reason to talk with an expert is because the tax code changes about as often as Madonna alters her looks. Plus, you need to know the tax ramifications of any financial gift you give.

"It's such an individual situation," says Wallem. "We run into boomers who have lost their jobs or are in a career change. Many of them are worried about having enough to retire on. That's really their main focus. There are others who have done well financially and are looking at estate taxes and asking how they can pass their assets on to the next generation."

The bottom line: Financially help your grandchildren as early as you can. No matter what you contribute, let it come from the heart.

A Groovy Kind of Love

Becoming the Best Grandparent

Face Time

If you want to be a super twenty-first-century nana or papa, you must give your grandchildren two treasured gifts. No, not a six-foot-tall teddy bear from FAO Schwarz or a Pentium II, 300 megahertz, nine-gig PC with a rewritable CD-ROM. The gifts we're talking about are the same ones that good grandparents have been sharing with their kids' kids since the beginning of civilization. And they cost nothing.

"The two best things you can give to your grandchildren are love and time," declares Dr. T. Berry Brazelton. "The danger is in trying to seduce your grandchildren by giving them bigger or more expensive gifts, hoping they'll remember you better. They aren't going to remember you for things like that anyway. The great reward of being a grandparent is that your grandchildren, like your mother and father, love you for yourself—and for no other reason."

Giving grandkids your love is easy. Giving them your time . . . well, that can be tough, especially since you need to spend time with each one of them alone.

If your grandchildren are typical, they're experiencing much less face time with their parents than you did with yours when you were a kid. Out of necessity, most of today's parents are leading Mad Hatter, beat-the-clock lives and must opt for "quality time" squeezed in somewhere between the tuna casserole, the dirty laundry, the sales report revisions, the boss's phone calls, and the kids' bath and bedtime.

Your grandchildren need your undivided attention, and with it your warm touch, knowing eyes, and sympathetic ears. In return, you'll get from them something more than just a sound bite.

In his Grandparent Study, Dr. Arthur Kornhaber found that grandchildren rarely mention things their grandparents had given them except for heirlooms. Instead, they talk about what their grandparents *did with them.*

"You really don't get to know the grandchildren unless you spend some time alone with them," says Dr. Susan Ginsberg, editor and publisher of the national newsletter *Work & Family Life.* "Kids usually don't interact with grandparents as much when the parents are around. You need to make an effort—however often it happens—to spend time alone with each kid so you both can get to know each other better."

That means, she says, spending time alone with one grandchild at a time. One on one. Just you and your grandchild. Not your spouse, not the other grandkids. Only the two of you.

It's the best way to build a deep, loving relationship and to make meaningful, lasting memories. If you need inspiration in pulling this off, press the rewind button in your head and replay those moments with your grandparents or significant elders who were important to you as a child. What was special about them in your life? What images and feelings are you experiencing in this rerun? How can you emulate or adapt those scenes to fit your role as a grandparent?

Kathy: *"Some of the moments I remember most with my Grandpa Clyde are the simplest ones. One time* *when I was five and visiting on the farm, he took me to town in his truck to the combine repair shop. He gave me a nickel for the Coke machine (the kind where the green bottle slid down the chute after you turned the handle). While I sat quietly drinking my Coke (which Mom never let me have), the welder fixed Grampa's broken combine part. This moment may not seem like much, but it has stayed with me for all these years. I think it's because it was the first time the two of us spent time together. We did lots of things together after that. We walked in the fields where he showed me how corn reproduces and pointed out the difference between a female and male melon blossom. He taught me how to bait a hook with a big juicy earthworm and use it to catch bass in his lake. When I was thirteen, he let me drive his truck around the barnyard. He didn't mind that the transmission cried out in protest during my futile attempts to shift gears.*

"What mattered was that I spent time with him— alone, not with my sister or my two brothers. I spent a lot of time alone with Grandma Lang too. My grandparents thought I—as well as each of their other twenty-five grandchildren—was special. Those were the happiest days of my childhood."

Grandmother Karen O'Connor, author of *Innovative Grandparenting*, wrote:

People of all ages are hungry for undivided personal time with one of their loved ones. Grandkids want to feel special and grandparents want to connect in a personal way.

But somehow life—the daily routine—gets in the way. It doesn't require money or even much time. It does require, however, that you be there, present to the child as a person who cares, who listens, who empathizes, who affirms, who is fun, and who is easy to be with.

That can take place over a pancake breakfast at a local diner or on the floor of your bedroom playing dolls. It can happen while you drive to the grocery store or hardware store or in a shared moment during a symphony or play. Whatever you choose, make sure it's something for just the two of you. Sitting on the park bench reading a newspaper while your grandchild plays alone in the sand at the park is not what I'm talking about. Dropping your grandchild off at a library event for children and then picking him up later doesn't count either.

No matter how busy you are, if you want to have a close relationship with your grandchildren, it's essential that you find ways to interact with them one at a time.

Here are four surefire, guaranteed, never-fail roles that you can play when you're alone with your grandchild:

The Playmate

"We need to get away from buying the newest Barbie doll every time we visit the grandchildren and getting only one hour's play out of it," says Jody Martin, curriculum specialist for the Children's World Learning Centers. "We need to get down on their level and just play with them."

Play whatever game or make-believe diversion your grandchild enjoys, says sociologist Susan Newman, a grandmother of five. Go into the child's world and do something that's of interest to her. If she wants to finger-paint, then finger-paint with her. If she wants to toboggan down Suicide Hill, do it. "It will be so meaningful," says Newman. "When my son was about four, his grandmother came to visit. He wanted to play with his toy newspaper truck, so she got down on the floor with him and she made little newspaper bundles and they loaded them in the truck and took them out. My son is grown now, and he still talks about that time with her."

It's never too early to start playing. If your grandchild is a baby, simply rock her, read or sing to her, take her out in a stroller. With a toddler or preschooler, sit on the floor and roll a ball back and forth; play tag, hide-and-seek, or horsey; make sand castles, play with her toys and dolls. With a slightly older child, try baking cookies together, swim, hike, blow bubbles, wrestle, jump rope, play board games, fish, do puzzles, tell jokes. The key is to have unadulterated fun. There doesn't have to be a reason to do it other than it seems like a great idea. Don't even have a hidden agenda of trying to teach her something. Follow the Beach Boys' philosophy: Fun, fun, fun!

> **Carrie (Maw Maw) Dulcette:** *"Every time I see my grandson, I have to get down on my hands and knees and play grizzly bear with him."*

> **Gran Nan:** *"Bree loves to sing and I do too. So we're always singing the most nonsensical songs—most of them made up on the spot."*

One of the joys of playing with our grandsons Chad and Danny is watching the world through their eyes. We see their sheer happiness over popping a floating soap bubble, picking up a lost shiny penny, or stomping in a puddle. We hear their squeals of discovery over seeing an ant carry a crumb, feeling the vibrations of a purring cat, or listening to the tones from touching a phone's keypad.

"Parents are so concerned with molding the child's mind and helping her grow up that they don't take the time to see things through her eyes," says Dr. Perry Buffington. "Grandparents don't want to rush grandkids into growing up too fast because they enjoy playtime with the kids."

Find out what your grandchild likes to do—then do it with her.

The Friend

Appreciate all your grandchild's strengths and flaws. She needs someone who's there to give her unqualified support and understanding. Offer encouragement and compassion. Lend an ear, listen to her fears and anxieties, and offer advice when asked. Let her feel so comfortable with you that she could tell you anything. She can count on you to be there in good times and bad. If her self-esteem is shaky because of constant criticism from parents or teachers, you need to build up her ego. You can best take on this role of a friend if you let her get close to you.

"Fun is a fine thing in a grandparent but the key is approachability," says Dr. Buffington. "You need to be there for her. Grandparents typically are far better listeners than parents. Your ability to be a friend doesn't have any strings attached."

> **Linda (Mimi) Gray:** *"I'm amazed not only at what comes out of her [granddaughter's] mouth, but what comes out of mine when we're together. We talk about everything. She's only five and already she knows my life story."*

When you talk to your grandchild, you need to be involved enough in her life so that you know what questions to ask, says Newman. "That's when you need the parents to help you. Talk to them first so you know what's happening in your grandchild's life—what's going on in her play group or in preschool. Then you can have a fulfilling conversation that relates to her. You'll be able to ask the right questions."

To get more out of the relationship, ask your grandchild open-ended questions, suggests Martin. "If you ask questions that can be answered in one word, that's what you'll likely get. If you ask, 'How are you?' or 'How was the movie?' you'll probably hear 'fine.' It's better to ask questions like, 'What was your favorite part of the movie?' and follow up with 'Why?' It leads to so many other questions and a nice conversation. Another way to get her talking is to say something like, 'Tell me about the animals you saw at the zoo.'"

Also, it's important to talk about yourself, because that fosters a two-way relationship, Martin adds.

The Teacher

"Many grandparents feel they have to stock their houses with games and toys for their grandchildren when children actually learn so many other things just by being with their grandparents," says Dr. Kornhaber.

Do you have a skill or a hobby? Cooking, car repair, computers, painting, music, sailing, horseback riding, candle-making, surfing? Whatever pastime you enjoy, introduce it to your grandchild. Perhaps your passion will rub off on her. So often, the younger generation learns from the older generation.

"As mentors, grandparents can spark a grandchild's imagination, providing motivation and inspiration by just being there," says Dr. Kornhaber. "These lessons often have a lifelong influence." The Grandparent Study reported that knowledge, skills, and attitudes acquired from grandparents stuck more permanently than things grandchildren picked up from other sources.

> **Ray (Papa) Villwock:** *"I passed down to my sons my love for fishing but not to the extent that I had hoped. However, as a grandfather, I can spend more time fishing with my grandkids and pass down to them my passion for the sport."*

Keri (Grams) Lytle: *"My hobby is pottery, and Maddie, who's four, likes to play with clay and mold it into intriguing shapes. She has some great talent. I'm helping her learn how to throw pots."*

Sandi (Grammy) Kingman: *"I love to bake. My grandmother taught me and now I'm teaching my grandchildren. I'm teaching each one to make his or her own specialty—strawberry-rhubarb pie for Staci and pecan pie for Robby."*

For most young children the chance to observe the world is a great learning experience. You can show your grandchild the wonders of the most common, ordinary, and everyday things in life.

"Go on an outing together," suggests Martin. "Spend time in nature just listening and observing. Smell flowers, look for bugs, notice the weather. Your grandchild will ask lots of questions for you to answer."

Picnics are a wonderful time to share nature with your grandchild. Watching ducks paddle in a pond, clouds float overhead, or squirrels gather nuts helps teach her a respect for the world around her.

Nana Lana: *"I like to take the grandkids out at night and snuggle on a blanket in a nearby field and gaze at the stars. I make up stories about the constellations and occasionally we make wishes when we see shooting stars."*

You can teach more than just skills or the world around us. You can teach by example—by setting the standards for the family in morals and values, by practicing your spiritual beliefs, and by honoring your family's culture and traditions.

"As a grandparent, you can teach lessons that go back several generations," says Dr. Buffington. "Because you are aware of your own mortality, you become more concerned with binding the generations. You become a better teacher of traditions and morality than the parents. The kids are watching you to some degree more than they are watching their parents.

"For some of us, that may mean cleaning up our act. Better late than never. It makes a difference."

The Family Historian

When you show grandchildren their family roots, they learn they are part of a larger, living entity. You provide them with a new perspective in understanding how things of today link up with the past. Above all, you help them learn about the family history, their ancestors, and the origin of the family name.

"Grandparents are the family archivists, providing grandchildren with a link to the past through stories of relatives long dead as well as passing on family ways, rites, and rituals," says Dr. Kornhaber.

This role takes some effort. Collect photos of your parents and grandparents and put them in an album. That way you can point out to your grandchildren from whom they got their wiry hair, their musical voice, their fiery temper.

If you haven't already, collect family heirlooms and things from your own past. Make videos of any living elderly relatives, tape oral histories, gather any family journals and letters. Let the kids rummage through the attic, basement, or storage shed. (You might want to get rid of the hookah and lava lamp. What are you keeping those for anyway?) Children find the most wonderful treasures in these places. You can spend countless hours pulling out memorabilia and telling fascinating stories attached to each special item.

"Kids love it when they look at photo albums and hear stories about their parents when they were kids," says Martin.

It's healthy to show off the pictures of you with the long hair and the tie-dyed clothes, Dr. Buffington adds. "It's no different than George Washington's white wig. It was a statement of the times. Tell them about the Vietnam War. Tell them how your generation started Earth Day and advocated more freedom of mind and choice, and fueled the women's movement."

> **Tom (Grandpa) Andersen:** *"I have a collection of front pages of important events that happened during my life—JFK's assassination, Neil Armstrong walking on the moon, Nixon resigning. I will use them as starting points for me to talk about my life to my grandkids when they're old enough to understand."*

> **Kathy:** *"I'm marking all the heirlooms that I have from my parents, grandparents, and great-grandparents. I'm sticking labels underneath the items so that my grandkids will know where these things came from."*

> **Kirk Leiter:** *"Every family photo is on computer disk so hopefully it will always be there for all my grandchildren to enjoy. I've made several copies."*

You serve as a human video of the family's personal saga of experiences and events (some of which, no doubt, you'll want to edit out). You get to explain how your life was affected by Haight-Ashbury, the Chicago Eight trial, the Arab oil embargo, whatever.

Making Time

You say you don't have time to be a playmate, friend, teacher, and historian to each grandchild? Find the time. No, *make* the time. What can be more important than playing a major role in the life of a child? Don't be one of those boomers who's trying to jam more "me time" into an already crammed schedule because you're freaked out that life is passing you by too quickly. If you don't get involved with your grandchildren right now, what will pass you by is your opportunity to make a positive impact in their lives.

If you have the time for one more set on the clay courts or one more vodka and tonic at happy hour, you can make the time for your grandchild. Sometimes it takes a little planning or flexibility to create opportunities to be with a little one.

"Being with your grandchild doesn't require as much time as you think," says Newman. "Children envision time differently than adults do. A half hour or hour may seem short to us, but to a child who is enjoying what she's doing, that time is expanded for her."

You can always make time. For example, if you're at a family gathering, sneak away after the meal with one of the grandkids and go for a walk—alone. Or take her to a nearby park for a few minutes so she can play on the swings. "You might be amazed at how special a time you'll both have even in a short span of time," says Newman.

"If you have simple chores to do, do them together. Perhaps you could get a child-size rake for her and let her help you rake the yard. Take her to the grocery store with you because it can be a wonderful learning experience. You can point out shapes, colors, and sizes, and, depending on her age, even some basic math. Take her with you to the bank, post office, gas station, construction site, or wherever you need to go for your errands. Just being together is the important thing."

Dr. Ginsberg sometimes takes her granddaughter to the office or to exercise class so she can see what her nana does for work and for fun. "It allows me to spend more time with her. Anything you can do to involve your grandchildren in your life, do it."

If possible, find ways you can alter your work schedule so you can be with your grandchild for a special event such as a birthday party or a recital. Maybe you can finish the management report on your PC at home, swap shifts with a fellow employee, or get someone to cover for you at the store.

To get the most out of your time together, become a nana or papa who specializes in something fun, Newman suggests. "Tie it in with something you need to accomplish or that you really like to do. For example, if you enjoy gardening, then become the gardening grandparent.

"Be a specialist so that your grandchildren think of you in a special way. Don't make yourself the gift-buying grandparent; make something of yourself. My five grandchildren think of me as the activity grandmother. We're always doing something—hunting for four-leaf clovers, taking a ride on a train, building a snowman, carving pumpkins. Those short blocks of time like that can leave lasting impressions.

"The best way to make the most of your limited time is to plan ahead. Figure out what you're going to do before you get together with your grandchild. It doesn't have to be anything complex. The more interaction, the more lasting the impression. Those moments are going to stand out in her mind.

"It doesn't matter what the activity is, just be totally involved and focused with your grandchild, which some parents have such difficulty doing because they are spread so thin. If you have only a half hour, do what she wants to do.

"If you come into her house, sit down, turn on the TV while she's in the room, that's not quality time. It's only good time if you are paying attention to her and there's interaction.

"When you're together, by the way, take lots of photographs to build a memory bank in her mind. Toddlers aren't necessarily going to remember all the fun they had with you."

If possible, set up a video camera and record the whole afternoon. Children love to watch themselves over and over again. The tape also will capture that special day forever.

Reading to Your Grandchild

Of all the activities that a grandparent can do, we believe that one of the most important and rewarding is reading to your grandchild. Everyone benefits. You both spend precious time together, and you help her develop a love of books and the written word. Reading builds a foundation for future success in school and acts to prevent her from overdosing on TV and videos. Children who have been read to become better readers.

Martin and the Children's World Learning Centers offer these tips to help you foster a positive reading experience for your grandchild:

- Remember that just spending time reading to her is more important than what is read.
- Eliminate distractions (TV, radio, phone, etc.) when you read to her.
- Find a comfortable place to read—a couch, easy chair, bed, or beanbag chair.
- Help her select the book she wants to read.
- Provide her with varied books of interest to her. Says Martin, "Books that make sounds and have rhythm or show pictures of babies and animals appeal to infants. Toddlers enjoy books with textured pictures and with objects they can name. Sesame Street and Barney stories are popular with preschoolers, as are books about other children. Five- and six-year-olds are intrigued with magical stories, fairy tales, and books about dinosaurs and animals."
- Don't just open the book and start reading. "There's so much more to learn from a book than just reading it. Spend time talking about it first. Discuss the cover, show her the name of the author and explain that the

person wrote it. Flip through the book and look at the pictures and have her point out the colors and objects. Ask her such things as, 'Can you find all the squares in the picture?' 'How many times does the word *the* appear on this page?'"

- Let her participate in the reading by turning pages, saying words, lifting flaps, and asking questions.
- Discuss the book after you've read it. "Ask her, 'How would you end the story?' 'What character would you like to be?' Suggest that she draw a picture about the story."
- Use the book to spur conversation with her about such topics as day care, friends, likes and dislikes, fun experiences, pets, etc.
- Keep books handy and stored in such a way that your grandchild can easily find the book she wants to read.

Creating Traditions and Rituals

As a grandparent, you should maintain or create family traditions and rituals, say the experts. In a changing world of uncertainty, traditions and rituals provide the family—especially children—with something regular, consistent, reliable, cherished, and predictable to look forward to.

Carrie (Maw Maw) Dulcette: *"On New Year's Day, the whole family jumps into our pond—no matter how cold the temperature is. Even the little ones, after the age of four, go in. This will be Sean's first time. He'll finally realize what a crazy family he's born into."*

"Rituals and traditions help form a family's identity," says family expert Dr. Gregory Sanders. "They provide important opportunities for families to express their strengths and build their relationships. I have my students write about their family traditions and rituals. Many students say these are very powerful and positive mechanisms for keeping their family going. They particularly refer to Thanksgiving and Christmas as the times their families most often experience their rituals and traditions.

"Once a ritual is established, it causes some family disagreements if anyone tries to alter it in any way. However, we're not as good at practicing them as we have been in the past and we're losing out because of that."

Dr. Buffington agrees. "Traditions are more important than ever before," he says. "People crave traditions and cherish these moments. Kids remember moments. If a child knows that every December fifth we are going out to cut down a Christmas tree because it's a family tradition, then that consistency provides comfort to him.

"If your family adopted a tradition, chances are your adult child is teaching it to your grandkid. It's a linkage you have. A good grandparent will take the traditions that have already been implemented and try to make them better. If your family does not have any traditions or rituals, then for God's sake, make up some. Your job as a grandparent is to create moments. It's essential. You must have something as a link to the past. One of the reasons people want these links is that the present is so tenuous."

It's also important to foster or create a ritual that's between you and your grandchild—a special activity that just the two of you do together on certain occasions.

Allan: *"Chad and I have started to collect waterfalls. Every summer we will hike to a different waterfall and have our photo taken there. I'll have a different ritual with Danny when he gets a little older."*

Ray (Papa) Villwock: *"I took Max to the Florida Marlins Opening Day game when he was five months old, and he's been to every Opening Day game since. He's still too young to fully appreciate it. But when he's grown up, he'll be able to say that since he was born, he's been to every Marlins' Opening Day with his grandfather."*

Spoiling Your Grandchild

A classic bumper sticker reads: "Grandparents and grandchildren get along so well because they both have the same enemies." We nanas and papas get to conspire with our grandkids to do all the little things that Mom and Dad normally would frown upon.

We don't worry about grandkids staying up past bedtime, gobbling too many sweets, or wearing mismatched clothes. We get to concentrate on the fun stuff. This is our big reward for all those car pools, scout meetings, orthodontic appointments, PTA bake sales, Little League games, and piano lessons that dominated our conversations (and, for many of us, our lives) when we were raising our kids. This is the payback for all the times we had to say no, to send our kids to their rooms, to make them do their chores. Now we get to say yes to our grandkids, to indulge their every whim, and basically to have a blast.

Glen (Pee Paw) Reed: *"A moment with my grandsons brightens a week at a time and explains all those moments when my parents fawned over my kids."*

"Some parents envy the relationship their children have with the grandparents," says Dr. Kornhaber. "Behavior that might be regarded as spoiling a child may, from another viewpoint, be recognized as simply an extension of the affection that many grandparents lavish on their grandchildren."

> **Michelle (Grammy) Davies:** *"I can sum up my role as a grandmother in a few words: 'To spoil my grandkids rotten!'"*

You'll probably get some flak from the parents for spoiling their child, but, hey, what can they do? Ground you? When we baby-sat Chad for five days while his parents took a much-needed vacation before Danny was born, we indulged him, no doubt about it. Okay, so maybe we went a little overboard, because on the first day Chad returned home, his mother needed to send him to "time-out" three times. But Allison and Dan didn't complain about our spoiling him. They knew that was a small price to pay for their getaway. In fact, they sent us a gift certificate to an upscale restaurant as a thank-you. Although we were pleased with the thoughtful gesture, didn't they know that we would've *paid* them to baby-sit for Chad?

How Do You Want to Be Remembered?

So, what kind of nana or papa will you be? You can probably best answer that question by asking yourself another question: How do I want my grandchildren to remember me? Once you answer that, all you have to do is turn that thought into reality.

> **Ray (Papa) Villwock:** *"How do I want to be remembered? As the papa who was a lot of fun to be with and loved life."*

> **Jane (Nana) Trebble:** *"I want to be the grandma who gave her grandkids warm memories and a happy childhood."*

David (Pop-Pop) Pilgrim: *"The hip-hop Pop-Pop."*

Nana on the Net: *"I intend to be the grandparent who can provide my grandchildren with stability in times of crisis."*

Sue (Nana) Crawford: *"I want to be remembered as the fun grandma."*

Jane (Grandmom) Whitfield: *"To be someone who is genuine, sincere, and supportive of my grandchildren."*

Michelle (Grammy) Davies: *"The grammy who can make anything the grandkids want—from cookies to toys—magically appear."*

Carrie (Maw Maw) Dulcette: *"I'm fixing to be the craziest, silliest, funnest grandma this family has ever had."*

Kathy: *"I want to be a great big warm human security blanket for my grandkids."*

Allan: *"For my grandkids, I hope to be a mix of Soupy Sales, Mr. Wizard, Buffalo Bob, Pinky Lee, Captain Kangaroo, and Bozo the Clown."*

Appendix

Who Can I Turn To?
Resources for Nanas and Papas

Web Sites

The following Web sites are aimed at grandparents looking for informative articles, book reviews, advice, links, resources, on-line discussion groups, freebies, FAQs, on-line games and activities to do with grandchildren, free e-cards, and/or gift catalogs for grandchildren:

- Caring Grandparents of America
  http://www.uconnect.com/cga
- Foundation for Grandparenting
  http://www.grandparenting.org
- Grandparents Parenting . . . Again
  http://members.aol.com/granyanie/grg.html
- Grands Place (Grandparents and Special Others Raising Children)
  http://www.grandsplace.com
- Off Our Rockers
  http://www.sonic.net/thom/oor

- For My Grandchild
  http://www.mygrandchild.com

- KinderGuide
  http://www.kinderguide.com

- Third Age
  http://www.thirdage.com/grand

- Family Web
  http://www.familyweb.com

- Disney's Family.com
  http://www.family.disney.com

- ParentsPlace
  http://www.parentsplace.com

- ALA Great Sites
  http://www.ala.org/parentspage/greatsites

- Senior-Site
  http://seniors-site.com/grandpar/g_articl.html

- The Grandparent Guidebook
  http://www.gfn.org/p90s/Grandparents/allindex.html

- Child Welfare League of America
  http://www.cwla.org

- Generations United
  http://www.gu.org

- Divorcenet
  http://www.divorcenet.com

(Web site addresses often change. If you have trouble accessing any of these addresses, type in the name of the organization in your search engine for the latest address.)

Newsletters

- *Parenting Grandchildren: A Voice for Grandparents*

    To get on the mailing list for the Grandparent Information Center's free semiannual newsletter about issues affecting grandparents who raise grandchildren, write to:

    Parenting Grandchildren: A Voice for Grandparents
    601 E Street, NW
    Washington, DC 20049
    phone: (202)434-2296
    fax: (202)434-6474

- *Vital Connections*

    For a free copy of this quarterly newsletter from the Foundation for Grandparenting, send a self-addressed, legal-size envelope with fifty-two cents postage to:

    Foundation for Grandparenting
    7 Avenida Vista Grande
    Suite B7-160
    Santa Fe, NM 87505
    phone: (505)466-1336
    e-mail: gpfound@trail.com
    Web site: http://www.grandparenting.org

- *Off Our Rockers*

    This casual newsletter offers quips and anecdotes from fellow grandparents, book reviews, and other interesting information. Contact:

    Off Our Rockers
    PO Box 17516
    West Palm Beach, FL 33416-7516
    e-mail: elaines@bellsouth.net
    Web site: http://www.sonic.net/thom/oor

- *Work & Family Life*

    This monthly four-color newsletter provides information and practical advice on a wide range of family, job, and health issues that affect the working parent and grandparent. For further information:

    > *Work & Family Life*
    > 317 Madison Avenue
    > Suite 517
    > New York, NY 10017
    > phone: 1-800-278-2579 or (212)557-3555
    > fax: (212)557-9479
    > e-mail: workfam@aol.com

Organizations

The following groups seek ways to strengthen the bond between grandparents and grandchildren:

- The Foundation for Grandparenting

    > 7 Avenida Vista Grande
    > Suite B7-160
    > Santa Fe, NM 87505
    > phone: (505)466-1336
    > e-mail: gpfound@trail.com
    > Web site: http://www.grandparenting.org

- Child Welfare League of America

    > 440 First Street NW
    > Third Floor
    > Washington, DC 20001-2085
    > phone: (202)638-2952
    > e-mail: webweaver@cwla.org
    > Web site: http://www.cwla.org

• Generations United

440 First Street NW
Suite 310
Washington, DC 20001
phone: (202)662-4283
e-mail: gu@cwla.org
Web site: http://www.gu.org

The following are national support groups that offer advice, encouragement, resources, and other information for those nanas and papas who are raising grandchildren:

• The Grandparent Information Center (GIC)

601 E Street, NW
Washington, DC 20049
phone: (202)434-2296
fax: (202)434-6466

• Grandparents Who Care

One Rhode Island Street
San Francisco, CA 94103
phone: (415)865-3000
fax: (415)865-3099

• Grandparents Parenting . . . Again

1014 Hopper Avenue
Suite 221
Santa Rosa, CA 95403
phone: (707)522-0242
fax: (707)541-0754
e-mail: granyanie@aol.com
Web site: http://members.aol.com/granyanie/grg.html

- Grands Place (Grandparents and Special Others Raising Children)
    - 112 Jennings Drive
    - Summerville, SC 29483
    - phone: (803)875-6720
    - fax: (803)871-1886
    - e-mail: scgram@grandsplace.com
    - Web site: http://www.grandsplace.com

- National Coalition of Grandparents
    - 137 Larkin Street
    - Madison, WI 53705
    - phone: (608)238-8751
    - fax: (608)238-8751

- Grandparents as Parents (GAP)
    - PO Box 964
    - Lakewood, CA 90714
    - phone: (562)924-3996
    - fax: (714)828-1375
    - e-mail: linstead@oxy.edu

- R.O.C.K.I.N.G./Raising Our Children's Kids: An Intergenerational Network of Grandparents, Inc.
    - PO Box 96
    - Niles, MI 49120
    - phone: (616)683-9038

For information concerning grandparenting legal issues:

- Grandparents Rights Organization
    - 555 S. Old Woodward Avenue
    - Suite 600
    - Birmingham, MI 48009
    - phone: (248)646-7191
    - fax: (248)646-9722

Grandchild Safety

For further information on toy safety, childproofing, and other child safety concerns:

- U.S. Consumer Product Safety Commission (CPSC)
  Washington, DC 20207
  phone: 1-800-638-2772 or (301)504-0580
  e-mail: info@cpsc.gov
  Web site: http://www.cpsc.gov

For the free thirty-two-page booklet *Your Child's Health and Safety* (it's geared to parents, but it applies to nanas and papas as well), contact:

- Children's World Learning Centers
  Health and Safety Booklet
  573 Park Point Drive
  Golden, CO 80401
  phone: (303)526-3261
  e-mail: cwlc@www.childrensworld.com
  Web site: http://www.childrensworld.com

Grandparent-Grandchild Travel

For information about attending a weeklong "grand" camp experience for grandparents and their grandkids only:

- Grandparent-Grandchild Summer Camp
  Sagamore Historic Adirondack Great Camp
  PO Box 146
  Raquette Lake, NY 13436
  phone: (315)354-5311

For grandparents looking for one of several fun, educational, and fascinating escorted vacations with their grandchildren:

- Grandtravel

  6900 Wisconsin Avenue
  Suite 706
  Chevy Chase, MD 20815
  phone: 1-800-247-7651; in Maryland, (301)986-0790
  e-mail: grandtrvl@aol.com
  Web site: http://www.grandtrvl.com

To learn more about a multigenerational European vacation experience:

- Grandparents' Houseparty

  Country Cottages
  2300 Corporate Boulevard, NW
  Suite 236
  Boca Raton, FL 33431
  phone: 1-800-674-8883
  e-mail: cottages@worldnet.att.net
  Web site: http://www.europvacationvillas.com

Recommended Reading

Books on Grandparenting

- *Contemporary Grandparenting* by Arthur Kornhaber, M.D. (Sage Publications, 1996). A scholarly but readable and informative look at today's grandparents.

- *Grandparent Power!* by Arthur Kornhaber, M.D., and Sondra Forsyth (Crown Publishers, 1994). Insightful tips and observations from the grandparenting guru.

- *The Essential Grandparent* by Dr. Lillian Carson (Health Communications, 1996). Excellent grandparenting tips from a psychotherapist.

- *Little Things Mean a Lot* by Susan Newman (Crown Publishers, 1996). Gift book crammed with good ideas about being better grandparents.

- *Innovative Grandparenting* by Karen O'Connor (Concordia Publishing House, 1995). Grandparenting advice with a spiritual point of view.

- *Sunny Days & Starry Nights* by Nancy Fusco Castaldo (Williamson Publishing, 1996). A collection of hands-on nature activities for very young children.

- *Grandloving: Making Memories with Your Youngest Grandchildren* by Sue Johnson and Julie Carlson (Fairview Press, 1996).

Children's Books That Feature Grandparents

The following books are appropriate for children from ages two through eight:

- *Coco Can't Wait* by Taro Gomi (Viking, 1985). The story of a Japanese grandmother and granddaughter who can't wait to see each other.

- *When I Am Old with You* by Angela Johnson (Orchard Books, 1993). A beautiful story of an African-American grandfather and granddaughter and how they spend summer together.

- *A Kiss for Little Bear* by Else Holmelund Minarik (Harper Trophy, 1984). The story of how a kiss between grandchild and grandmother affects all those around them.

- *Love You Forever* by Robert Munsch (Firefly Books, 1995). The story of how a mother's love carries across two generations.

- *A Chair for My Mother* by Vera Williams (Greenwillow, 1987). A grandmother helps her granddaughter save enough money for her mother who works long hours.

- *Tell Me a Story, Mama* by Angela Johnson (Orchard Books, 1992). An African-American mother tells her daughter stories of her own childhood with the child's grandparents and how the grandparents loved and raised her.

- *Something from Nothing* by Phoebe Gilman (Scholastic Books, 1993). A beautiful Jewish folktale of a grandfather who makes a blanket for his grandson and what happens to the blanket in daily life in the shtetl where they live.

- *More, More, More* by Vera Williams (Mulberry Books, 1996). A rich and affectionate story of how family members, including a grandmother, show their love for toddlers by playing with them.

- *Abuela* by Arthur Dorros (Puffin, 1997, and Demco Media, 1997). A young girl takes a wonderful fanciful trip with her grandmother around Manhattan.

- *Thunder Cake* by Patricia Polacco (Paper Star, 1997, and Demco Media, 1997). A grandmother helps her granddaughter with the child's fear of thunderstorms.

- *Annie and the Old One* by Miska Miles (Little Brown, 1985, and Demco Media, 1985). A Native American girl comes to terms with her grandmother's eventual death through a beautiful weaving that her grandmother is working on.

- *Staying with Grandma* by Eileen Roe (Simon & Schuster, 1989). A child's story about her visit to her grandmother's house in the country.

- *Stina* and *Stina's Visit* by Lena Anderson (Greenwillow, 1989, and Greenwillow, 1991). Tender stories of a young Norwegian girl who spends summer vacations with her grandfather on a small coastal island in Norway.

(The children's book list was prepared by the Erikson Institute for the Advanced Study of Child Development. In several cases, the books were published in different formats by other publishers than those listed here.)